SPATIAL REASONING WORKBOOK

Spatial Relations and Spatial Reasoning Practice

COMPLETE
TEST PREPARATION INC.
WWW.TEST-PREPARATION.CA

Copyright © 2021 by Complete Test Preparation Inc. ALL RIGHTS RESERVED. No part of this book may be reproduced or transferred in any form or by any means, graphic, electronic, or mechanical, including photocopying, recording, web distribution, taping, or by any information storage retrieval system, without the written permission of the author.

Notice: Complete Test Preparation Inc. makes every reasonable effort to obtain from reliable sources accurate, complete, and timely information about the tests covered in this book. Nevertheless, changes can be made in the tests or the administration of the tests at any time and Complete Test Preparation Inc. makes no representation or warranty, either expressed or implied as to the accuracy, timeliness, or completeness of the information contained in this book. Complete Test Preparation Inc. makes no representations or warranties of any kind, express or implied, about the completeness, accuracy, reliability, suitability or availability with respect to the information contained in this document for any purpose. Any reliance you place on such information is therefore strictly at your own risk.

The author(s) shall not be liable for any loss incurred as a consequence of the use and application, directly or indirectly, of any information presented in this work. Sold with the understanding, the author(s) is not engaged in rendering professional services or advice. If advice or expert assistance is required, the services of a competent professional should be sought.

The company, product and service names used in this publication are for identification purposes only. All trademarks and registered trademarks are the property of their respective owners. Complete Test Preparation Inc. is not affiliated with any educational institution.

Complete Test Preparation Inc. is not affiliated with the International Brotherhood of Electrical Workers, who are not involved in the production of, and do not endorse this publication.

We strongly recommend that students check with exam providers for up-to-date information regarding test content.

Version 8.5 April 2022
Published by
Complete Test Preparation Inc.
Victoria BC Canada
Visit us on the web at https://www.test-preparation.ca
Printed in the USA

ISBN-13: 9781772453799

About Complete Test Preparation Inc.

Why Us?
The Complete Test Preparation Team has been publishing high quality study materials since 2005, with a catalog of over 145 titles, in English, French and Chinese, as well as ESL curriculum for all levels.

To keep up with the industry changes we update everything all the time!

And the best part?
With every purchase, you're helping people all over the world improve themselves and their education. So thank you in advance for supporting this mission with us! Together, we are truly making a difference in the lives of those often forgotten by the system.

Charities that we support -
https://www.test-preparation.ca/charities-and-non-profits/

You have definitely come to the right place.
If you want to spend your valuable study time where it will help you the most - we've got you covered today and tomorrow.

Feedback

We welcome your feedback. Email us at feedback@test-preparation.ca with your comments and suggestions. We carefully review all suggestions and often incorporate reader suggestions into upcoming versions. As a Print on Demand Publisher, we update our products frequently.

Contents

Getting Started

Folding and Rotating	**7**
Answer Key	22
Assembly	**24**
Answer Key	33
Line Following	**36**
Answer Key	45
Touching Blocks	**52**
Answer Key	59
Blocks	**62**
Answer Key	68
Cut Outs	**71**
Answer Key	80
Jigsaw	**82**
Answer Key	91
Matching Shapes	**94**
Answer Key	102
Visual Comparison	**104**
Answer Key	110
Conclusion	**112**

GETTING STARTED

CONGRATULATIONS! By deciding to practice for a spatial relations test, you have taken the first step toward acing the test! Of course, there is no point in taking this important examination unless you intend to do your best to earn the highest grade you possibly can. That means getting yourself organized and discovering the best approaches, methods and strategies to master the material. Yes, that will require real effort and dedication, but if you are willing to focus your energy and devote the study time necessary, before you know it you will be on your way to a brighter future!

Folding and Rotating

1. Ⓐ Ⓑ Ⓒ Ⓓ   21. Ⓐ Ⓑ Ⓒ Ⓓ
2. Ⓐ Ⓑ Ⓒ Ⓓ   22. Ⓐ Ⓑ Ⓒ Ⓓ
3. Ⓐ Ⓑ Ⓒ Ⓓ   23. Ⓐ Ⓑ Ⓒ Ⓓ
4. Ⓐ Ⓑ Ⓒ Ⓓ   24. Ⓐ Ⓑ Ⓒ Ⓓ
5. Ⓐ Ⓑ Ⓒ Ⓓ   25. Ⓐ Ⓑ Ⓒ Ⓓ
6. Ⓐ Ⓑ Ⓒ Ⓓ   26. Ⓐ Ⓑ Ⓒ Ⓓ
7. Ⓐ Ⓑ Ⓒ Ⓓ   27. Ⓐ Ⓑ Ⓒ Ⓓ
8. Ⓐ Ⓑ Ⓒ Ⓓ   28. Ⓐ Ⓑ Ⓒ Ⓓ
9. Ⓐ Ⓑ Ⓒ Ⓓ   29. Ⓐ Ⓑ Ⓒ Ⓓ
10. Ⓐ Ⓑ Ⓒ Ⓓ   30. Ⓐ Ⓑ Ⓒ Ⓓ
11. Ⓐ Ⓑ Ⓒ Ⓓ   31. Ⓐ Ⓑ Ⓒ Ⓓ
12. Ⓐ Ⓑ Ⓒ Ⓓ   32. Ⓐ Ⓑ Ⓒ Ⓓ
13. Ⓐ Ⓑ Ⓒ Ⓓ   33. Ⓐ Ⓑ Ⓒ Ⓓ
14. Ⓐ Ⓑ Ⓒ Ⓓ   34. Ⓐ Ⓑ Ⓒ Ⓓ
15. Ⓐ Ⓑ Ⓒ Ⓓ   35. Ⓐ Ⓑ Ⓒ Ⓓ
16. Ⓐ Ⓑ Ⓒ Ⓓ   36. Ⓐ Ⓑ Ⓒ Ⓓ
17. Ⓐ Ⓑ Ⓒ Ⓓ   37. Ⓐ Ⓑ Ⓒ Ⓓ
18. Ⓐ Ⓑ Ⓒ Ⓓ   38. Ⓐ Ⓑ Ⓒ Ⓓ
19. Ⓐ Ⓑ Ⓒ Ⓓ   39. Ⓐ Ⓑ Ⓒ Ⓓ
20. Ⓐ Ⓑ Ⓒ Ⓓ   40. Ⓐ Ⓑ Ⓒ Ⓓ

1. When the two longest sides touch what will the shape be?

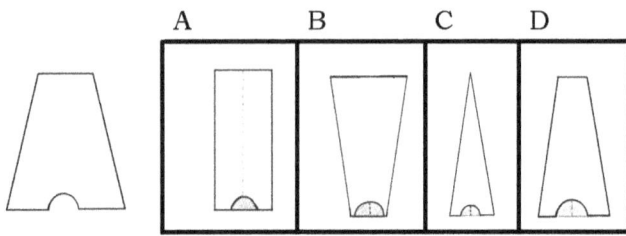

2. When folded, what pattern is possible?

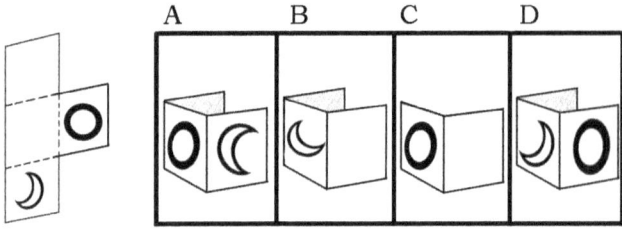

3. When folded into a loop, what will the strip of paper look like?

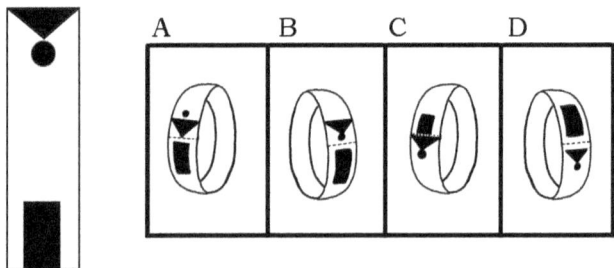

4. Which of the choices is the same pattern at a different angle?

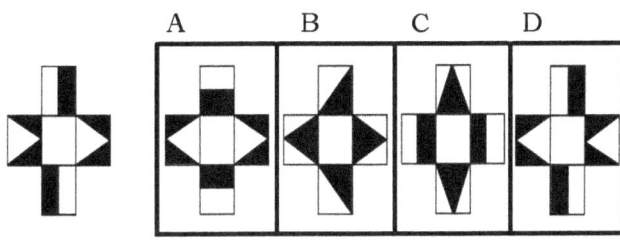

5. When put together, what 3-dimensional shape will you get?

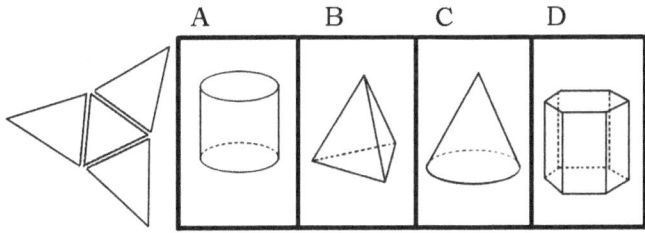

6. When folded, what pattern is possible?

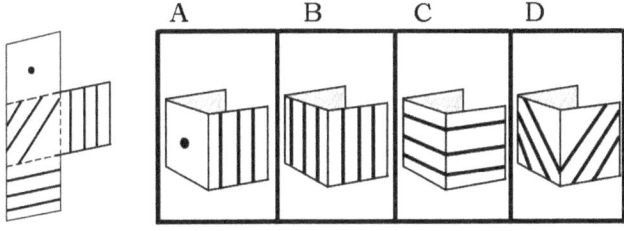

7. When folded into a loop, what will the strip of paper look like?

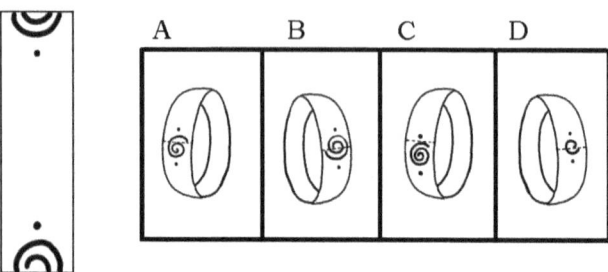

8. Which of the choices is the same pattern at a different angle?

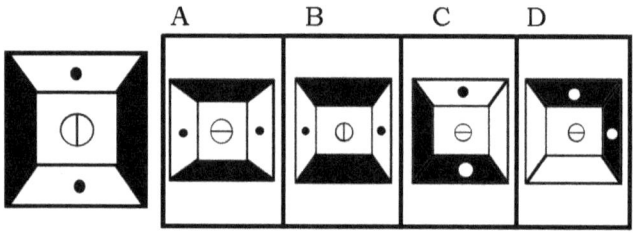

9. When folded, which shape will you get?

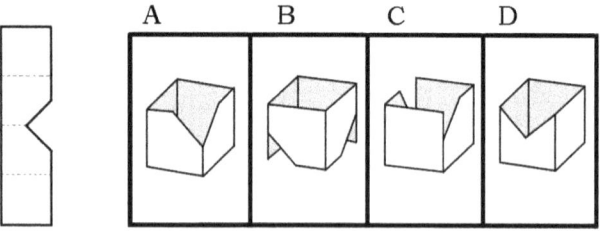

10. When folded, what pattern is possible?

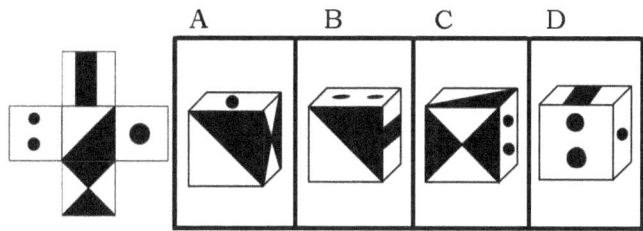

11. When folded, which shape is possible?

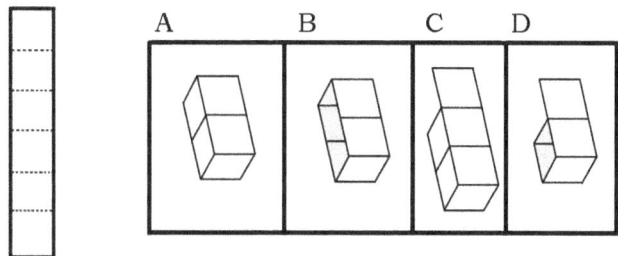

12. When folded, what pattern is possible?

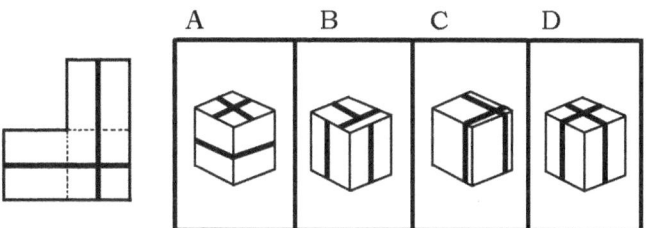

13. When folded into a loop, what will the strip of paper look like?

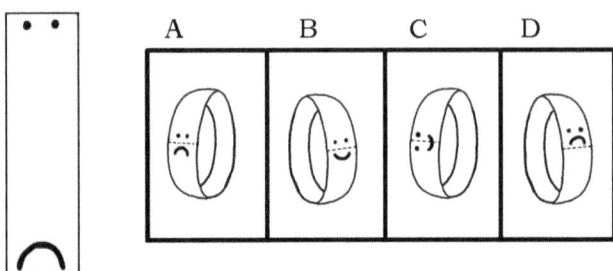

14. Which of the choices is the same pattern at a different angle?

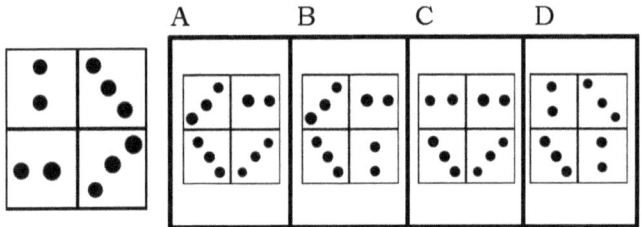

15. When folded along the dotted lines, which shape will you get?

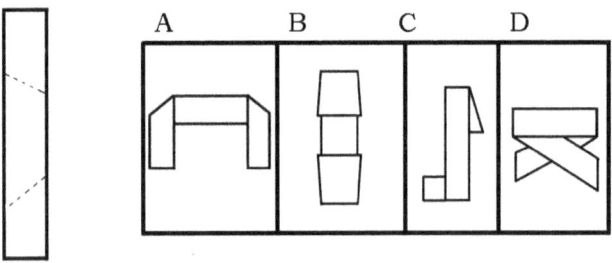

16. When folded, what pattern is possible?

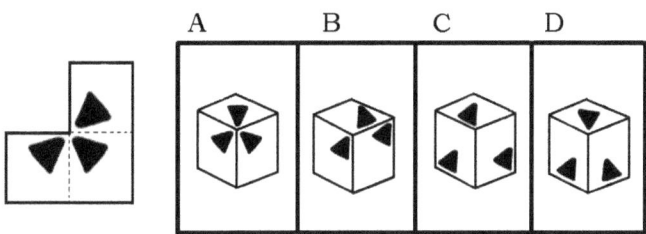

17. When folded into a loop, what will the strip of paper look like?

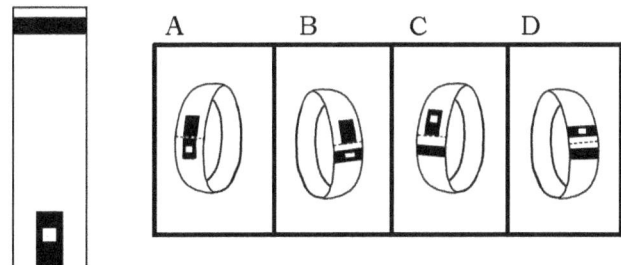

18. Which of the choices is the same pattern at a different angle?

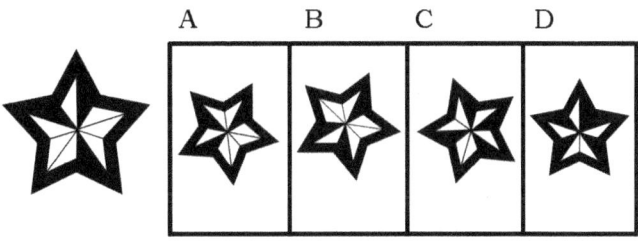

19. When folded along the dotted line, which shape will you get?

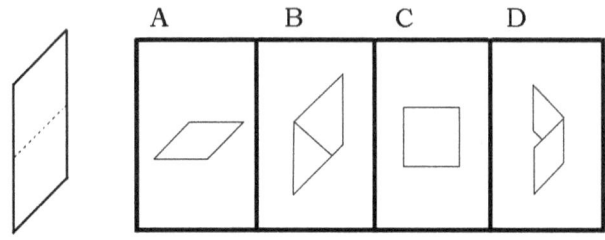

20. When folded, what pattern is possible?

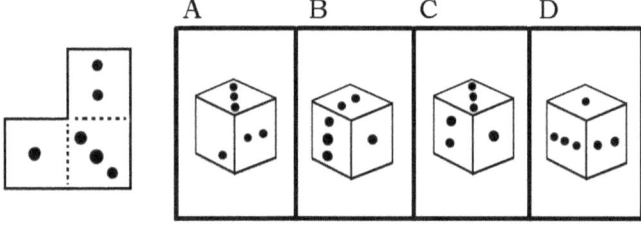

21. When folded, what pattern is possible?

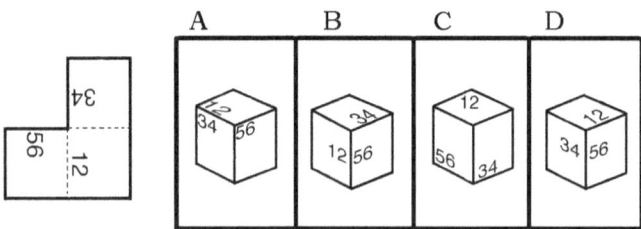

22. When folded into a loop, what will the strip of paper look like?

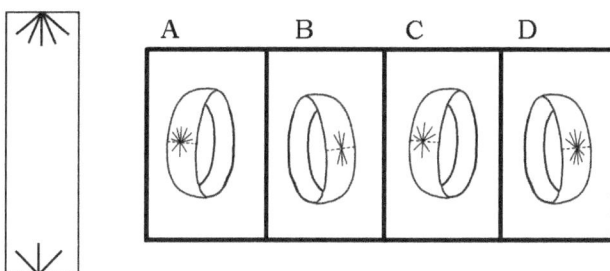

23. Which of the choices is the same pattern at a different angle?

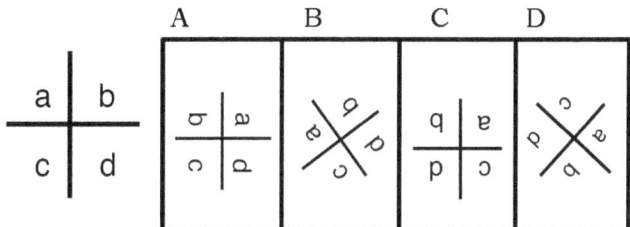

24. When folded, what pattern is possible?

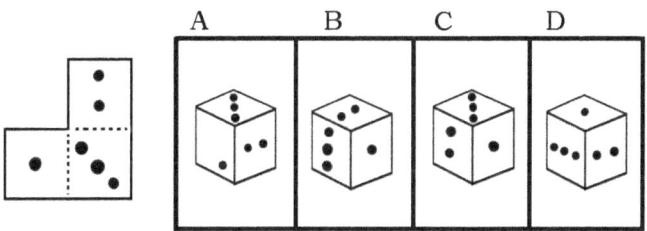

25. Which of the choices is the same pattern at a different angle?

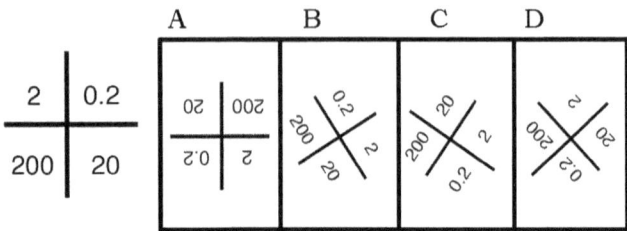

26. When folded along the dotted lines, which shape will you get?

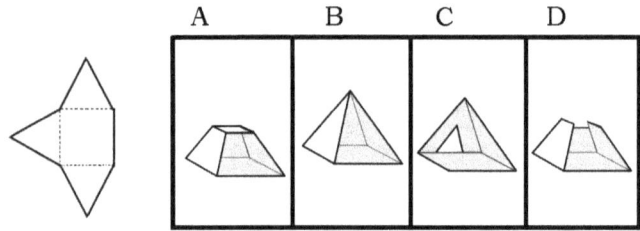

27. When folded, what pattern is possible?

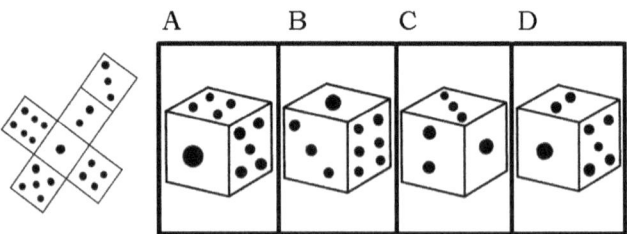

28. When folded into a loop, what will the strip of paper look like?

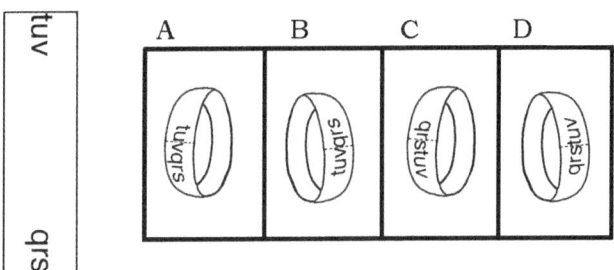

29. Which of the choices is the same pattern at a different angle?

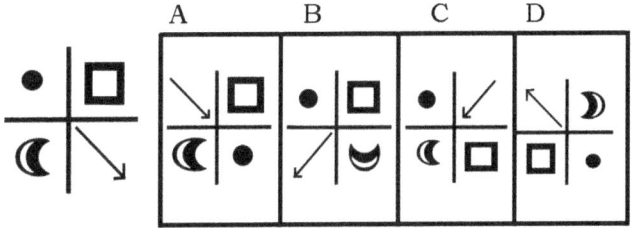

30. When put together, what 3-dimensional shape will you get?

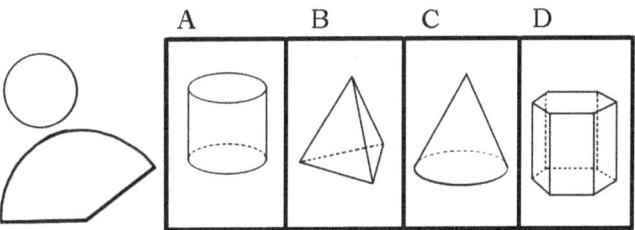

31. When folded, what pattern is possible?

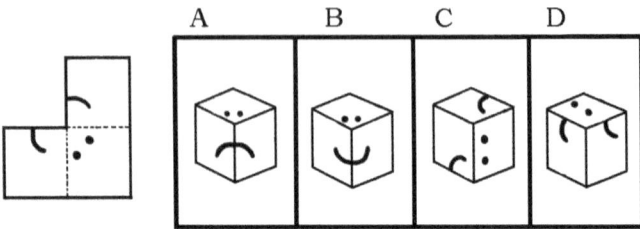

32. When folded, what pattern is possible?

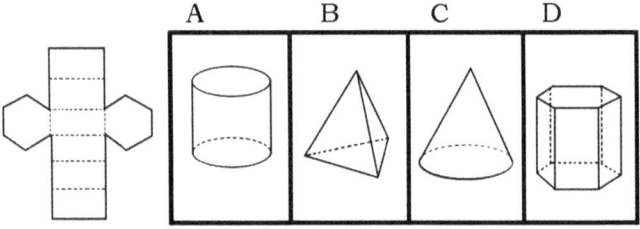

33. Which of the choices is the same pattern at a different angle?

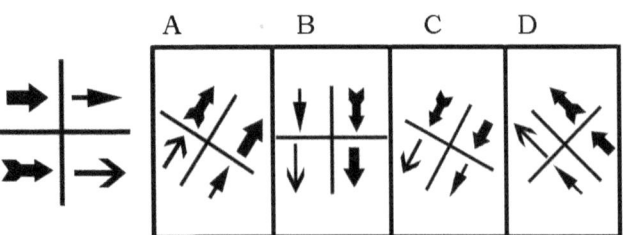

34. When put together, what 3-dimensional shape will you get?

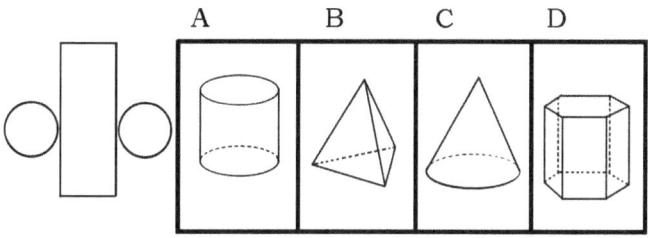

35. When folded into a loop, what will the strip of paper look like?

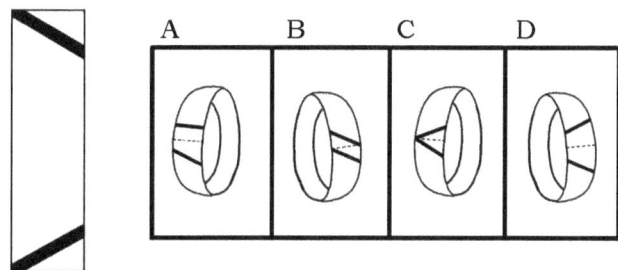

36. Which of the choices is the same pattern at a different angle?

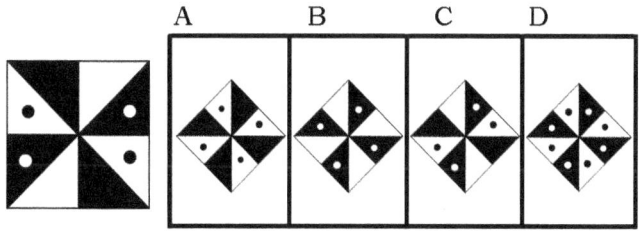

37. When put together, what 3-dimensional shape will you get?

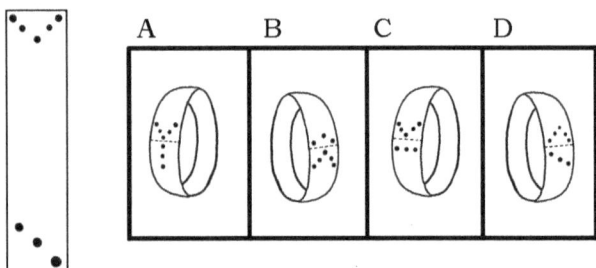

38. When folded into a loop, what will the strip of paper look like?

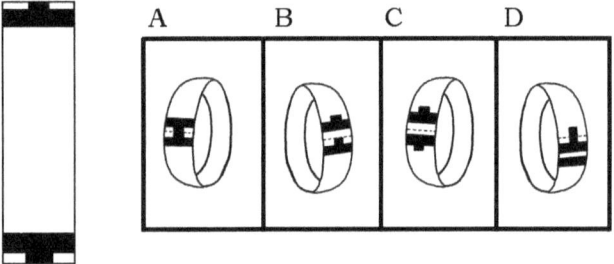

39. Which of the choices is the same pattern at a different angle?

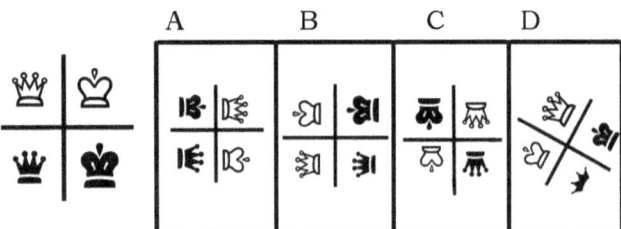

40. When folded into a loop, what will the strip of paper look like?

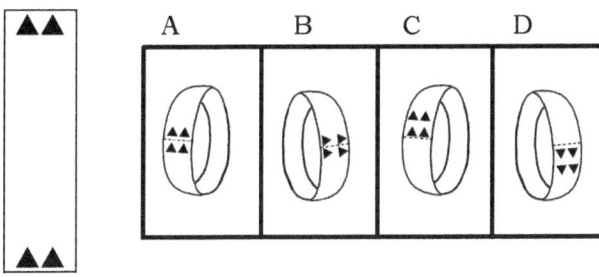

Answer Key

Folding and Rotating
1. D
2. A
3. C
4. B
5. B
6. C
7. B
8. A
9. A
10. A
11. B
12. D
13. B
14. B
15. A
16. A
17. C
18. B
19. D
20. C
21. D
22. C
23. D
24. C
25. A
26. B
27. A
28. D
29. D

30. C
31. B
32. D
33. C
34. A
35. C
36. C
37. D
38. A
39. B
40. A

Assembly

	A	B	C	D
1	○	○	○	○
2	○	○	○	○
3	○	○	○	○
4	○	○	○	○
5	○	○	○	○
6	○	○	○	○
7	○	○	○	○
8	○	○	○	○
9	○	○	○	○
10	○	○	○	○
11	○	○	○	○
12	○	○	○	○
13	○	○	○	○
14	○	○	○	○
15	○	○	○	○

1. Which figure represents the assembly of the following pieces?

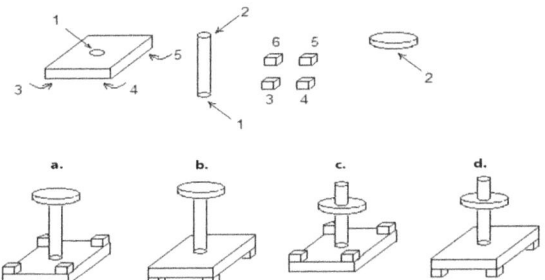

2. Which figure represents the assembly of the following pieces?

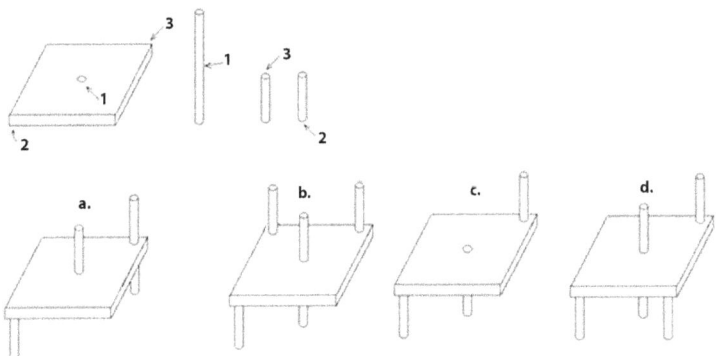

3. Which figure represents the assembly of the following pieces?

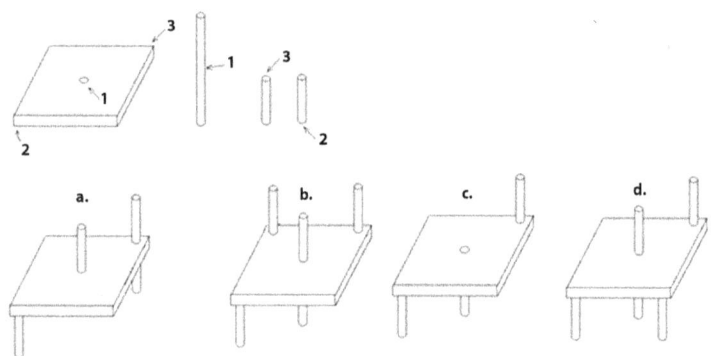

4. Which figure represents the assembly of the following pieces?

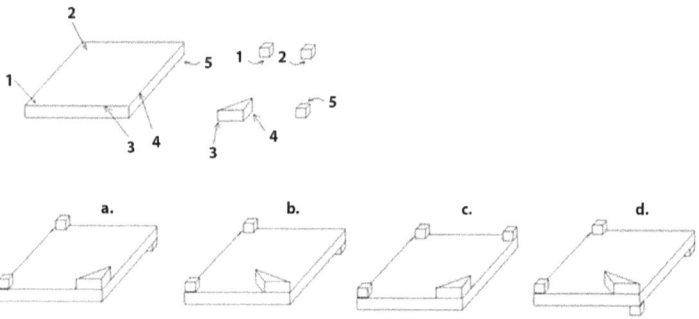

5. Which figure represents the assembly of the following pieces?

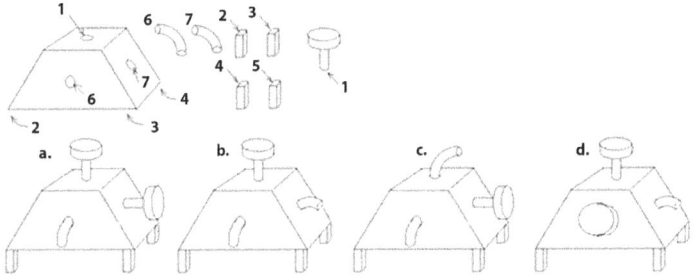

6. Which figure represents the assembly of the following pieces?

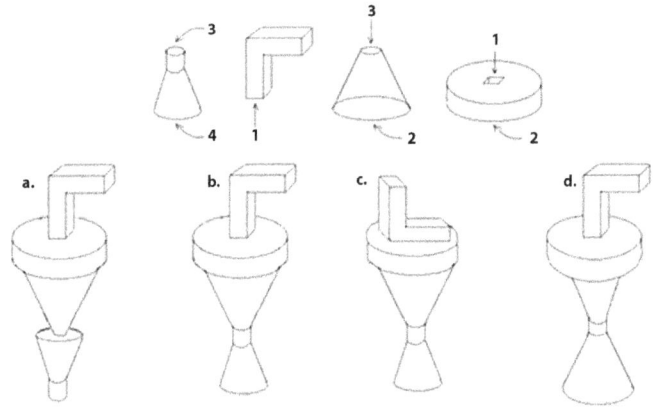

7. Which figure represents the assembly of the following pieces?

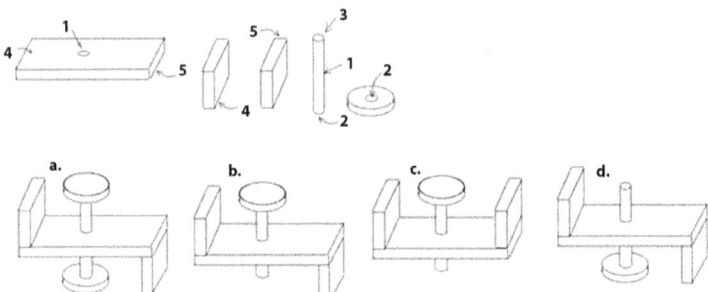

8. Which figure represents the assembly of the following pieces?

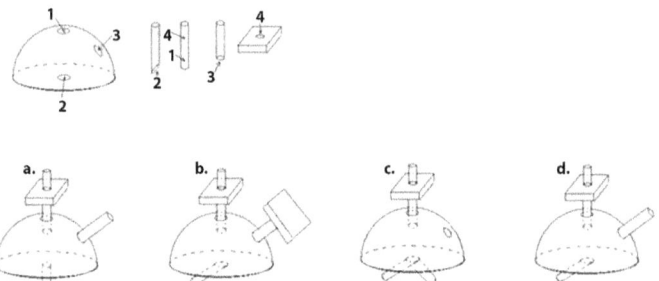

9. Which figure represents the assembly of the following pieces?

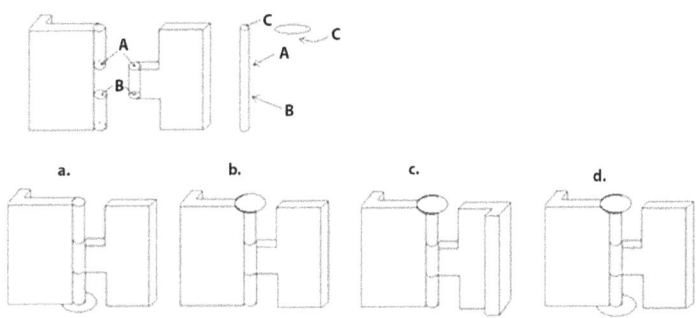

10. Which figure represents the assembly of the following pieces?

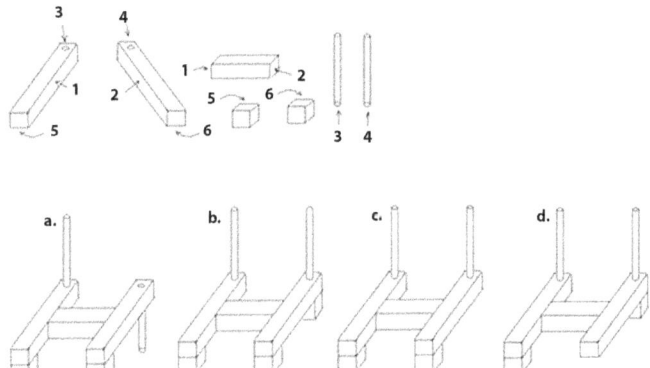

11. Which figure represents the assembly of the following pieces?

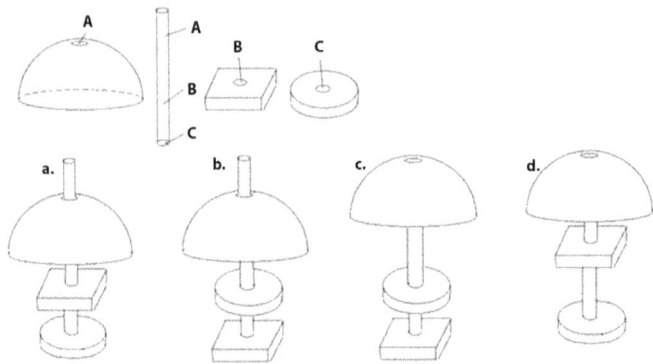

12. Which figure represents the assembly of the following pieces?

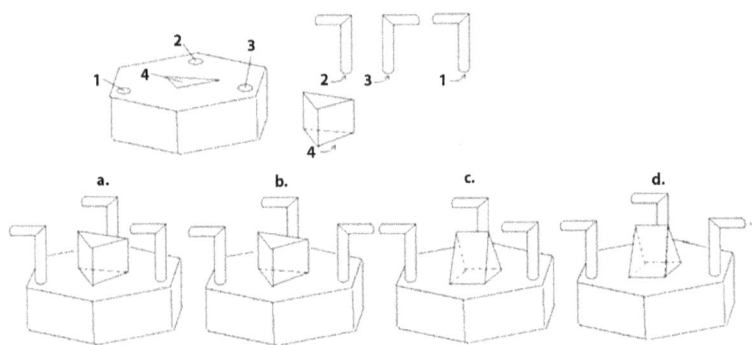

13. Which figure represents the assembly of the following pieces?

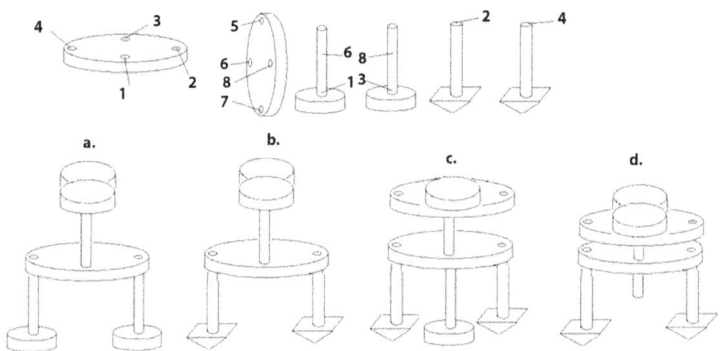

14. Which figure represents the assembly of the following pieces?

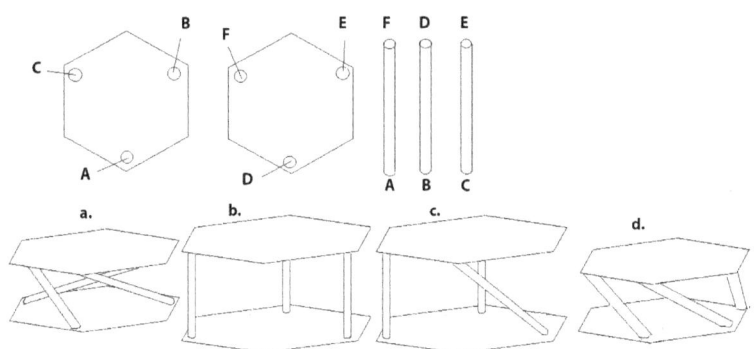

15. Which figure represents the assembly of the following pieces?

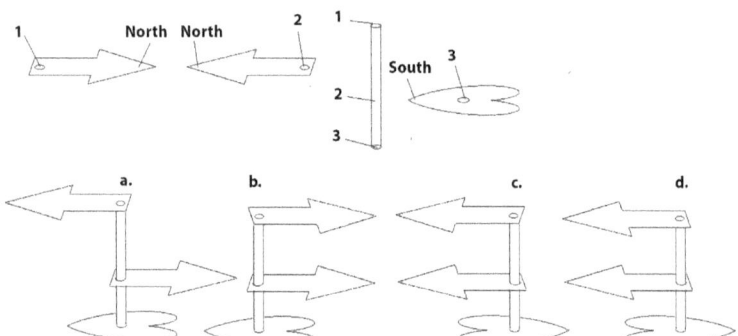

Answer Key

1. B
If two pieces have the same number at the position shown, it means that point is a junction point. Here, the cylindrical rod is at center of the rectangular platform, the small cubes are below the platform at its edges and the disc is above the rod.

2. D
If two pieces have the same number at the position shown, it means that point is a junction point. Here, the long rod is half above and half below the rectangular platform, and the short rods are one above and the other below the platform.

3. D
If two pieces have the same number at the position shown, it means that point is a junction point. Here, the rod connects the two wide wavy pieces and the two T-shapes are at the edges of the central rod.

4. A
If two pieces have the same number at the position shown, it means that point is a junction point. Here, all the small shapes are on the rectangular platform, where the triangular shape is on left-bottom corner and the three small cubes are at the other corners of the platform.

5. B
If two pieces have the same number at the position shown, it means that point is a junction point. Here, the hoses are at the central holes of the lateral faces of the platform, the screw-like shape is on top of the platform and the small cuboids act as legs.

6. B
If two pieces have the same number at the position shown, it means that point is a junction point. Following this rule, here will find that the correct assembly is shown at A.

7. D
If two pieces have the same number at the position shown, it means that point is a junction point. Here, the long rod is half above and half below the rectangular platform; the disc is at bottom of the rod, and the small rectangular shapes are in a vertical position at the extremities of the big rectangular platform, where the first is below the platform (the one on the right) and the other is above it (the one on the left).

8. D
If two pieces have the same number at the position shown, it means that point is a junction point. Here, the hose with one diagonal end is at the bottom of the half-sphere, while the hammer-like shape is on top.

9. B
If two pieces have the same number at the position shown, it means that point is a junction point. Here, the screw-like shape connects the two rectangular shapes with the head up.
Feedback for choice C
You may consider choice C, but one of the rectangular shapes is different from those given in the question.

10. C
If two pieces have the same number at the position shown, it means that point is a junction point. Here, there is a H-shaped object placed in the horizontal position and two vertical rods on the upper end of the H-shaped object.

11. A
If two pieces have the same number at the position shown, it means that point is a junction point. Here, there is a central rod, a half-sphere near the top of the rod, a rectangular-shaped object below the half of the rod and a disc at bottom of the rod.

12. B
If two pieces have the same number at the position shown, it means that point is a junction point. Following this rule, and maintaining the direction of the given shapes, you will notice that only B matches the description.

13. D

If two pieces have the same number at the position shown, it means that point is a junction point. Here, the screw-like shapes are placed vertically up, while the hammer-like shapes are vertically down. Also, there are two large discs at center of the platform.

14. A

If two pieces have the same number at the position shown, it means that point is a junction point. Here, the legs connect the positions shown in the upper platform with some points, which are shifted by two positions anti-clockwise.

15. D

If two pieces have the same number at the position shown, it means that point is a junction point. Here, the arrows and the upper part of the heart-shape must be in the same direction.

Line Following

	A	B	C	D
1	○	○	○	○
2	○	○	○	○
3	○	○	○	○
4	○	○	○	○
5	○	○	○	○
6	○	○	○	○
7	○	○	○	○
8	○	○	○	○
9	○	○	○	○
10	○	○	○	○
11	○	○	○	○
12	○	○	○	○
13	○	○	○	○
14	○	○	○	○
15	○	○	○	○
16	○	○	○	○
17	○	○	○	○
18	○	○	○	○
19	○	○	○	○
20	○	○	○	○

Questions 1 - 5 refer to the following diagram

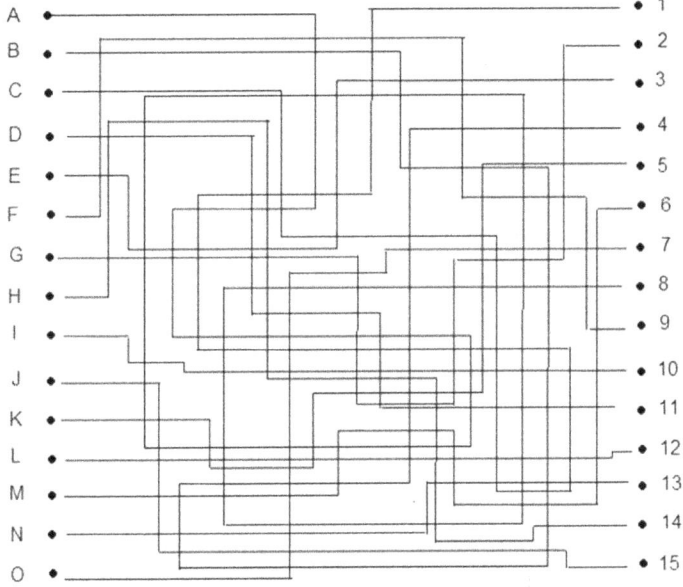

1. Which of the following is correct for the matching lines shown in the figure?

    a. A-1   E-5   I-14   L-12
    b. A-8   E-3   I-10   L-13
    c. A-8   E-3   I-10   L-12
    d. A-5   E-11   I-2   L-7

2. Which of the following is correct for the matching lines shown in the figure?

    a. B-4   F-9   J-15   M-6
    b. B-4   F-3   J-15   M-13
    c. B-6   F-9   J-12   M-7
    d. B-8   F-11   J-2   M-6

3. Which of the following is correct for the matching lines shown in the figure?

    a. C-4   G-9   K-15   N-6
    b. C-7   G-10   K-5   N-3
    c. C-1   G-2   K-12   N-7
    d. C-1   G-2   K-5   N-13

4. Which of the following is correct for the matching lines shown in the figure?

    a. D-5   H-10   L-11   O-13
    b. D-11   H-14   L-12   O-7
    c. D-5   H-7   L-10   O-11
    d. D-3   H-6   L-8   O-12

5. Which of the following is correct for the matching lines shown in the figure?

    a. A-4   C-11   M-12   L-13
    b. A-1   C-8   M-14   L-5
    c. A-8   C-1   M-6   L-12
    d. A-2   C-7   M-8   L-10

Questions 6 - 10 refer to the following diagram

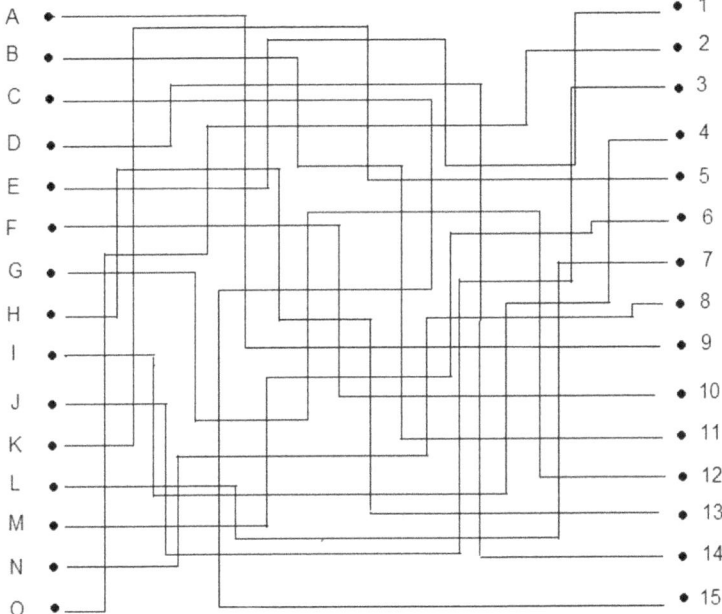

6. Which of the following is correct for the matching lines shown in the figure?

a.	D-4	G-12	I-14	K-5
b.	D-14	G-12	I-4	K-5
c.	D-4	G-10	I-6	K-12
d.	D-2	G-7	I-9	K-10

7. Which of the following is correct for the matching lines shown in the figure?

a.	A-9	E-1	M-6	N-8
b.	A-7	E-5	M-12	N-6
c.	A-9	E-1	M-6	N-12
d.	A-8	E-7	M-10	N-1

8. Which of the following is correct for the matching lines shown in the figure?

a. B-4	C-8	J-1	F-7
b. B-5	C-7	J-12	F-6
c. B-11	C-1	J-6	F-13
d. B-11	C-15	J-3	F-10

9. Which of the following is correct for the matching lines shown in the figure?

a. D-4	H-13	L-2	O-7
b. D-14	H-13	L-7	O-2
c. D-14	H-2	L-7	O-13
d. D-13	H-14	L-2	O-7

10. Which of the following is correct for the matching lines shown in the figure?

a. B-11	C-15	G-12	H-14
b. B-1	C-5	G-2	H-4
c. B-14	C-12	G-11	H-15
d. B-13	C-14	G-2	H-6

Questions 11 - 15 refer to the following diagram

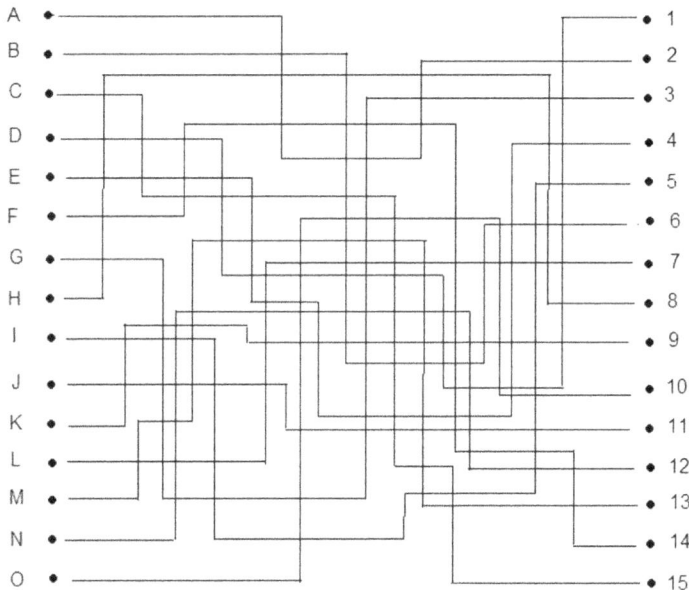

11. Which of the following is correct for the matching lines shown in the figure?

a.	A-2	B-5	C-6	D-1
b.	A-2	B-6	C-15	D-1
c.	A-4	B-13	C-2	D-5
d.	A-7	B-11	C-8	D-6

12. Which of the following is correct for the matching lines shown in the figure?

a.	A)	E-4	F-14	G-3	H-8
b.	B)	E-3	F-6	G-12	H-5
c.	C)	E-8	F-13	G-7	H-9
d.	D)	E-7	F-11	G-6	H-8

SPATIAL RELATIONS

13. Which of the following is correct for the matching lines shown in the figure?

a. I-5	J-7	K-9	L-11
b. I-5	J-7	K-11	L-9
c. I-5	J-11	K-9	L-7
d. I-7	J-11	K-8	L-9

14. Which of the following is correct for the matching lines shown in the figure?

a. M-13	N-12	O-10	E-4
b. M-12	N-13	O-14	E-9
c. M-5	N-11	O-9	E-7
d. M-7	N-11	O-7	E-9

15. Which of the following is correct for the matching lines shown in the figure?

a. G-3	B-12	D-6	F-14
b. G-2	B-13	D-4	F-9
c. G-5	B-14	D-6	F-3
d. G-3	B-6	D-1	F-14

Questions 16 - 20 refer to the following diagram

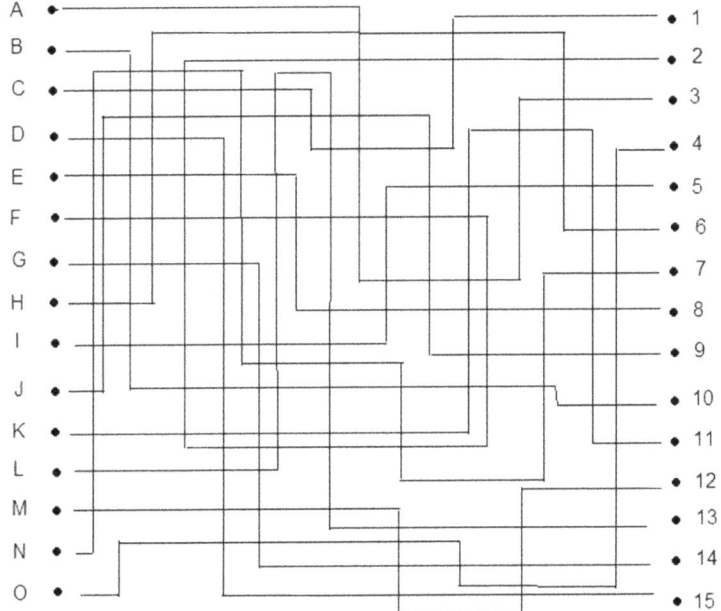

16. Which of the following is correct for the matching lines shown in the figure?

    a. A-3   B-10   C-1   D-15
    b. A-3   B-11   C-10   D-15
    c. A-3   B-13   C-12   D-5
    d. A-5   B-11   C- 3   D-15

17. Which of the following is correct for the matching lines shown in the figure?

    a. E-12   F-14   G-3   H-8
    b. E-13   F-6   G-12   H-6
    c. E-8   F-13   G-2   H-6
    d. E-8   F-2   G- 14   H-6

18. Which of the following is correct for the matching lines shown in the figure?

a.	I-5	J-7	K-9	L-11
b.	I-5	J-9	K-11	L-13
c.	I-5	J-11	K-9	L-13
d.	I-7	J-11	K-12	L-9

19. Which of the following is correct for the matching lines shown in the figure?

a.	M-13	N-12	O-4	L-7
b.	M-12	N-7	O-4	L-13
c.	M-15	N-11	O-13	L-4
d.	M-7	N-12	O-11	L-5

20. Which of the following is correct for the matching lines shown in the figure?

a.	C-1	F-2	D-15	M-12
b.	C-2	F-1	D-15	M-12
c.	C-5	F-12	D-2	M-3
d.	C-4	F-6	D-11	M-14

Answer Key

Diagram for Questions 1 - 5

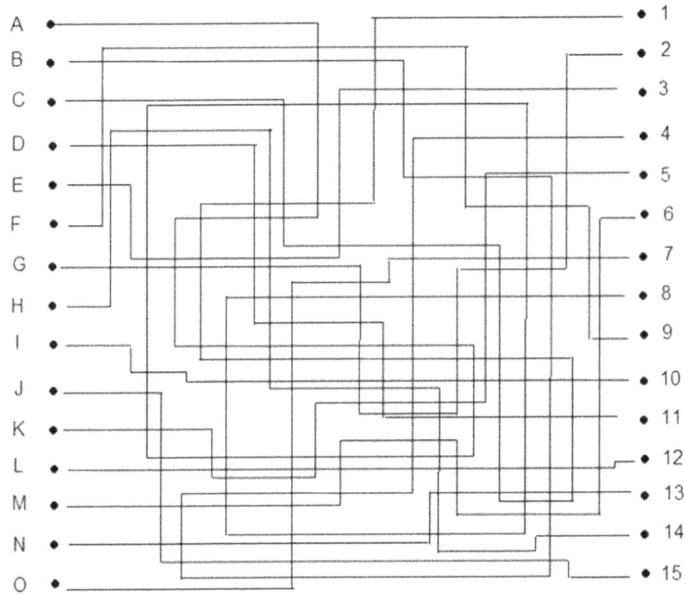

1. C
Carefully observing the lines, you will notice that the line starting from A ends at 8, the line starting from E ends at 3, the line starting from I ends at 10 and the line starting from L ends at 12.

2. A
Carefully observing the lines, you will notice that the line starting from B ends at 4, the line starting from F ends at 9, the line starting from J ends at 15 and the line starting from M ends at 6.

3. D
Carefully observing the lines, you will notice that the line starting from C ends at 1, the line starting from G ends at 2,

the line starting from K ends at 5 and the line starting from N ends at 13.

4. B
Carefully observing the lines, you will notice that the line starting from D ends at 11, the line starting from H ends at 14, the line starting from L ends at 12 and the line starting from O ends at 7.

5. C
Carefully observing the lines, you will notice that the line starting from A ends at 11, the line starting from C ends at 1, the line starting from M ends at 6 and the line starting from L ends at 12.

Diagram for Questions 6 - 10

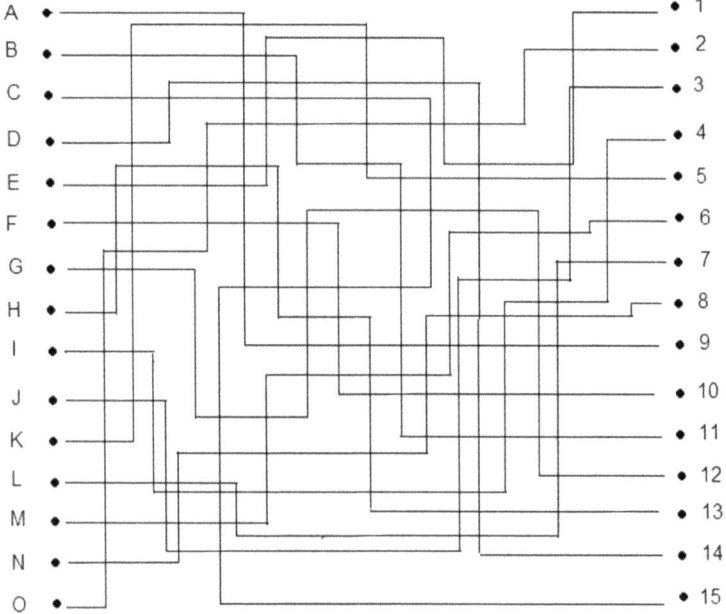

6. B
Carefully observing the lines, you will notice that the line starting from D ends at 14, the line starting from G ends at

12, the line starting from I ends at 4 and the line starting from K ends at 5.

7. A
Carefully observing the lines, you will notice that the line starting from A ends at 9, the line starting from E ends at 1, the line starting from M ends at 6 and the line starting from N ends at 8.

8. D
Carefully observing the lines, you will notice that the line starting from B ends at 11, the line starting from C ends at 15, the line starting from J ends at 3 and the line starting from F ends at 10.

9. B
Carefully observing the lines, you will notice that the line starting from D ends at 14, the line starting from H ends at 13, the line starting from L ends at 7 and the line starting from O ends at 2.

10. A
Carefully observing the lines, you will notice that the line starting from B ends at 11, the line starting from C ends at 15, the line starting from G ends at 12 and the line starting from H ends at 14.

Diagram for Questions 11 - 15

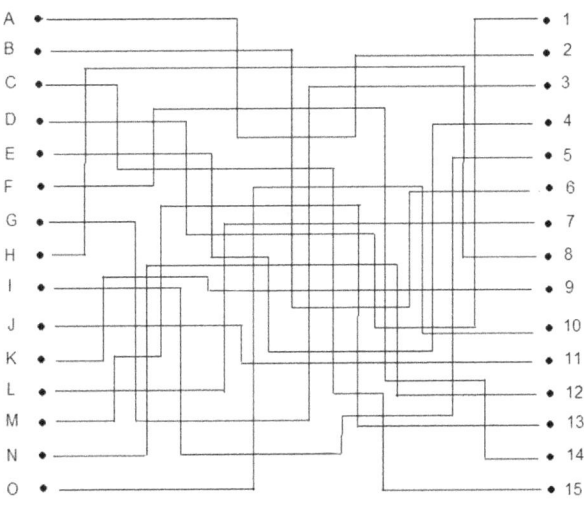

11. B
Carefully observing the lines, you will notice that the line starting from A ends at 2, the line starting from B ends at 6, the line starting from C ends at 15 and the line starting from D ends at 1.

12. A
Carefully observing the lines, you will notice that the line starting from E ends at 4, the line starting from F ends at 14, the line starting from G ends at 3 and the line starting from H ends at 8.

13. C
Carefully observing the lines, you will notice that the line starting from I ends at 5, the line starting from J ends at 11, the line starting from K ends at 9 and the line starting from L ends at 7.

14. A
Carefully observing the lines, you will notice that the line starting from M ends at 13, the line starting from N ends at 12, the line starting from O ends at 10 and the line starting from E ends at 4.

15. D
Carefully observing the lines, you will notice that the line starting from G ends at 3, the line starting from B ends at 6, the line starting from D ends at 1 and the line starting from F ends at 14.

Diagram for Questions 16 - 20

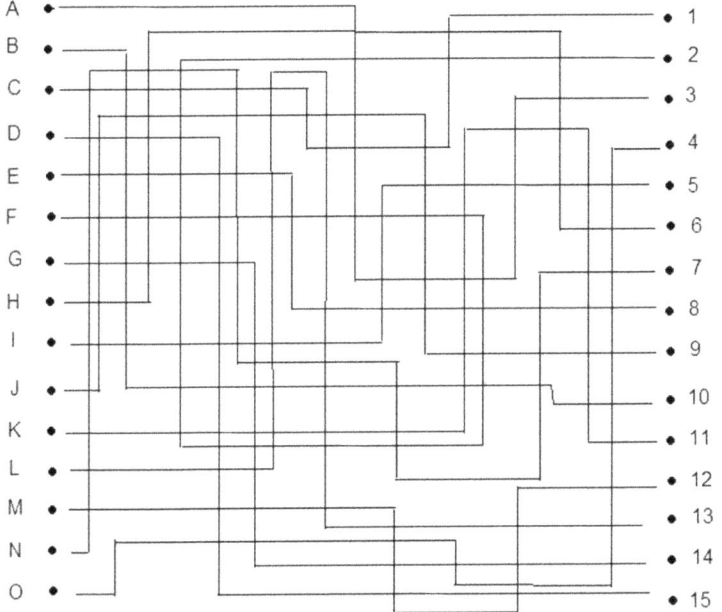

16. A
Carefully observing the lines, you will notice that the line starting from A ends at 3, the line starting from B ends at 10, the line starting from C ends at 1 and the line starting from D ends at 15.

17. D
Carefully observing the lines, you will notice that the line starting from E ends at 4, the line starting from F ends at 14, the line starting from G ends at 3 and the line starting from H ends at 8.

18. B
Carefully observing the lines, you will notice that the line starting from I ends at 5, the line starting from J ends at 9, the line starting from K ends at 11 and the line starting from L ends at 13.

19. B
Carefully observing the lines, you will notice that the line starting from M ends at 12, the line starting from N ends at 7, the line starting from O ends at 4 and the line starting from L ends at 13.

20. A
Carefully observing the lines, you will notice that the line starting from C ends at 1, the line starting from F ends at 2, the line starting from D ends at 15 and the line starting from M ends at 12.

Touching Blocks

	A	B	C	D
1	○	○	○	○
2	○	○	○	○
3	○	○	○	○
4	○	○	○	○
5	○	○	○	○
6	○	○	○	○
7	○	○	○	○
8	○	○	○	○
9	○	○	○	○
10	○	○	○	○
11	○	○	○	○
12	○	○	○	○
13	○	○	○	○
14	○	○	○	○
15	○	○	○	○

Questions 1 - 3 refer to the following diagram

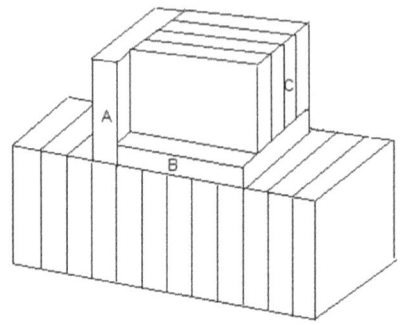

1. How many blocks is block A touching?

    a. 4
    b. 5
    c. 6
    d. 7

2. How many blocks is block B touching?

    a. 4
    b. 5
    c. 9
    d. 10

3. How many blocks is block C touching?

   a. 4
   b. 3
   c. 2
   d. 1

Questions 4 - 6 refer to the following diagram

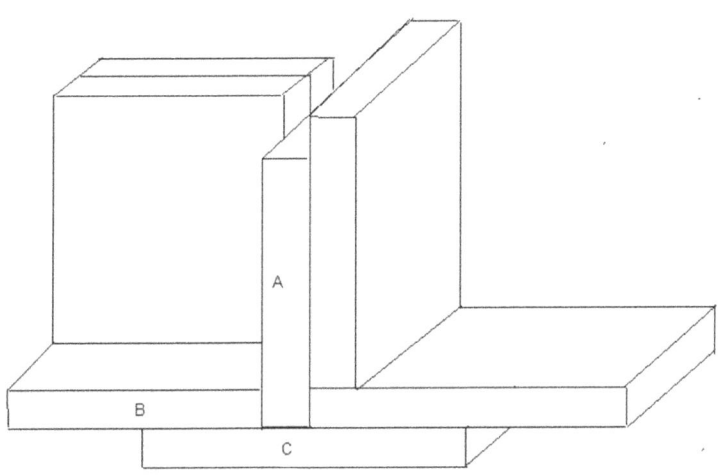

4. How many blocks is block A touching?

   a. 7
   b. 6
   c. 5
   d. 4

5. How many blocks is block B touching?

    a. 4
    b. 5
    c. 6
    d. 3

6. How many blocks is block C touching?

    a. 4
    b. 3
    c. 2
    d. 1

Questions 7 - 9 refer to the following diagram

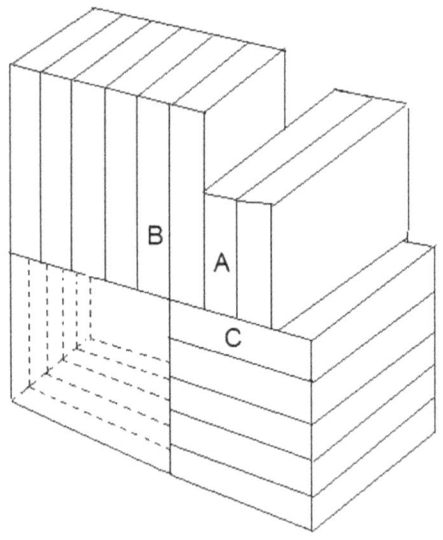

7. How many blocks is block A in the figure touching?
The blocks on the bottom-left side are transparent.

    a. 6
    b. 5
    c. 4
    d. 3

8. How many blocks is block B in the figure touching?
The blocks on the bottom-left side are transparent.

    a. 7
    b. 6
    c. 5
    d. 4

9. How many blocks is block B in the figure touching?
The blocks on the bottom-left side are transparent.

    a. 10
    b. 9
    c. 8
    d. 7

Questions 10 - 12 refer to the following diagram

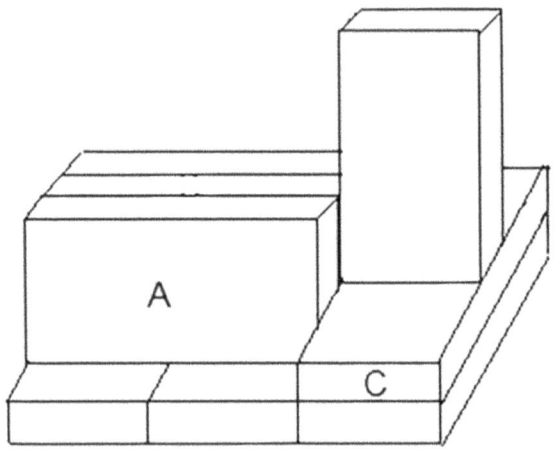

10. How many blocks is block A touching?

    a. 6
    b. 5
    c. 4
    d. 3

11. How many blocks is block B touching?

    a. 6
    b. 5
    c. 4
    d. 3

12. How many blocks is block C in the figure touching?

   a. 8
   b. 7
   c. 6
   d. 5

Questions 13 - 15 refer to the following diagram

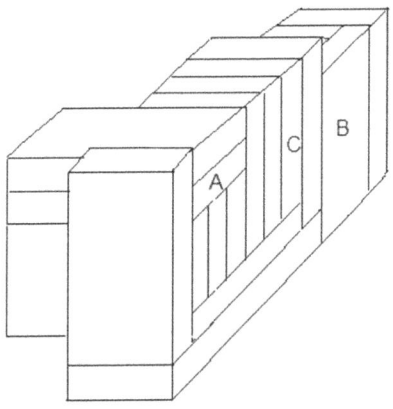

13. How many blocks is block A in the figure touching?

   a. 6
   b. 5
   c. 4
   d. 3

14. How many blocks is block B in the figure touching?

   a. 6
   b. 5
   c. 4
   d. 3

15. How many blocks is block C in the figure touching?

   a. 6
   b. 5
   c. 4
   d. 3

Answer Key

1. C
Block A touches 6 blocks (1 is below, 4 are lateral in vertical position and 1 is lateral in the horizontal position.

2. D
Block B touches 5 blocks below, 4 blocks above and one block laterally, i.e. in total 10 blocks.

3. A
Block C touches 4 blocks in total: 1 below, 2 blocks laterally on the wider side and one block laterally, in the narrower side.

4. B
Block A touches 6 blocks (1 is below, 2 are lateral in vertical position (narrow face), 2 are lateral in the horizontal position and one is lateral in the vertical position (wider side).

5. A
Block B touches 1 block below, 2 blocks above and one block laterally, i.e. in total 4 blocks.

6. B
Block C touches 3 blocks in total: all of them above it.

7. D
Block A touches 3 blocks in total: 2 are laterally placed and the other is below it.

8. A
Block B touches 5 blocks below and 2 laterally placed, i.e. in total 7 blocks.

9. B
Block C touches 1 blocks below, 5 laterally placed blocks, and 3 other blocks above it, i.e. 9 blocks in total.

10. C
Block A touches 4 blocks in total: 1 laterally placed, 2 below and 1 behind it.

11. B

Block B touches 5 blocks in total: 1 laterally placed, 2 below, 1 before and 1 behind it.

12. D

Block C touches 5 blocks in total: 3 laterally placed, 1 below and one above it.

13. A

Block A touches 6 blocks in total: 2 laterally placed, 3 below and 1 above it.

14. A

It is worth mentioning that the blocks are identical.
Block B touches 6 blocks in total: 3 laterally placed (2 vertical and 1 horizontal), and 3 are behind it.

15. D

Block C touches 2 blocks in total: 2 laterally placed, and another block below it.

Blocks

1. How many cubes are there in the figure?

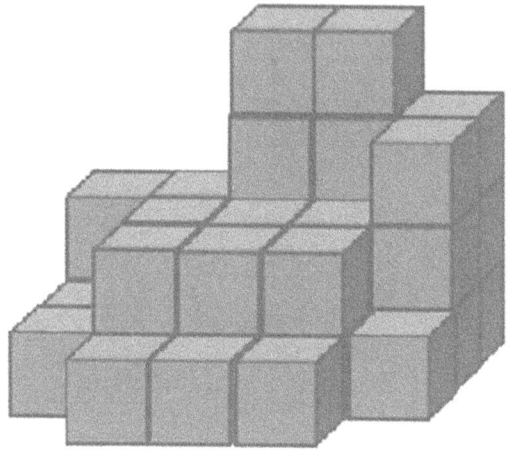

a. 30
b. 32
c. 35
d. 24

2. How many cubes are there in the figure?

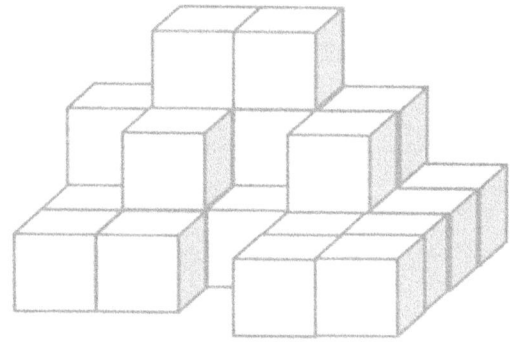

a. 30
b. 22
c. 15
d. 24

3. How many cubes must we add in the figure to form a perfect cube?

a. 55
b. 45
c. 70
d. 125

4. Which shape must we place to the right side of the figure to balance the weight of the system? All shapes are made by the same material.

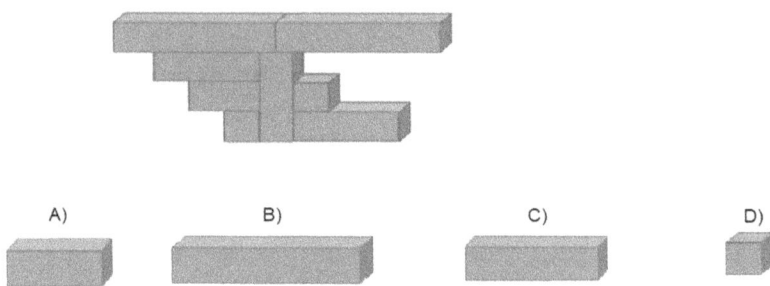

5. Which shape must we place on the existing figure to form a perfect square?

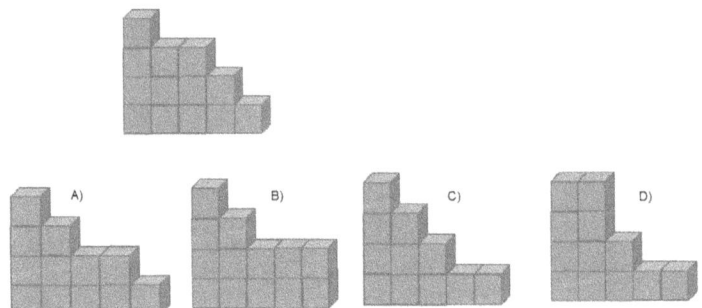

6. How many small cubes are missing in the figure to form a large perfect cube?

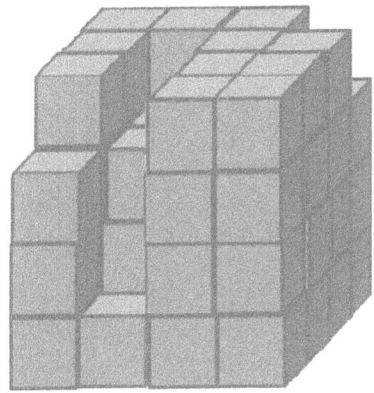

a. 6
b. 7
c. 8
d. 9

7. Which shape must we place on the existing figure to form a perfect cube?

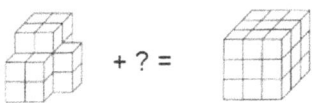

A) 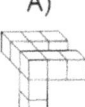   B)    C) 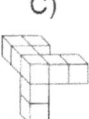   D)

8. Which shape must we place on the existing figure to form a perfect cube?

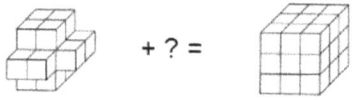

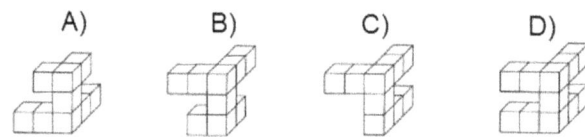

9. Which shape must we place on the existing figure to form a perfect cube?

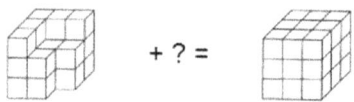

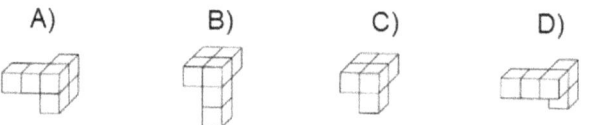

10. Which shape must we place on the existing figure to form a perfect cube?

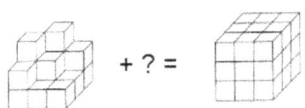

A)   B)   C)   D)

Answer Key

1. C
In the bottom row, there are 3 × 4 + 3 = 15 cubes.
In the next row, there are 2 + 3 + 3 + 3 + 1 = 12 cubes.
In the third row, there are 2 + 2 = 4 cubes.
In the upper row, there are only 2 cubes.
Thus, in total there are 15 + 12 + 4 + 2 = 33 cubes.

2. C
From the figure, you will see that there are 4 + 4 + 2 + 3 + 3 = 16 cubes in the bottom row, 2 + 1 + 2 + 1 = 6 cubes in the middle row and only 2 cubes in the upper row.

Thus, in total there are 16 + 6 + 2 = 24 cubes in the figure.

3. C
Since there are 5 cubes in the longest row, we need 5 × 5 × 5 = 125 cubes in total to form a perfect cube.

First, let's count the existing cubes. In the first row, there are 5 + 4 + 5 + 5 + 4 = 23 cubes.

In the second row, there are 5 + 3 + 4 + 4 + 1 = 17 cubes.
In the third row, there are 3 + 3 + 2 = 8 cubes.
In the fourth row, there are 3 + 3 + 1 = 7 cubes.

Thus, in total there are 23 + 17 + 8 + 7 = 55 cubes.

Hence, we must add 125 − 55 = 70 cubes to form a perfect big cube.

4. A
There are 4 kinds of shapes that are on the lateral sides of the vertical bar. These shapes vary in length. You may notice that on the right side, the second shortest shape is missing. Thus, it must be placed in that part to balance the system.

5. A
The existing figure has 4 rows and 5 columns, where not all of them are complete. To be a perfect square, it must have 5 × 5 dimensions.

From the figure, the first row is complete. In the second row one cube is missing, in the third row two cubes are missing, in the fourth row four cubes are missing and in the fifth row all 5 cubes are missing. There missing cubes must be filled with one of the shapes.

The only shape that fits the description is the first one.

6. B
A large perfect cube is formed when it has the dimensions 4 × 4 × 4.

The first row is complete, the second row has one cube missing, the third row has another cube is missing, and the fourth, upper row, 1 + 3 + 0 + 1 = 5 cubes are missing.

Hence, in total, 1 + 1 + 5 = 7 cubes are missing to form a perfect cube.

7. A
If you rotate the shapes in the choices by 90^0 clockwise, you will notice that the missing shape to form a perfect cube is the first one.

8. D
There are 5 missing cubes in the first row, 1 in the second and 5 in the third row. The only shape that fits the description is the fourth one. No rotation is needed.

9. B
There is one missing small square in the first row, one in the second and four squares in the third row. The only shape that fits the description is the second one. It does not need any rotation.

10. D
The first row does not have any missing cube. In the second row, only 3 cubes are missing at the closest corner. In the third row, 7 cubes are missing.

Cut Outs

	A	B	C	D
1	○	○	○	○
2	○	○	○	○
3	○	○	○	○
4	○	○	○	○
5	○	○	○	○
6	○	○	○	○
7	○	○	○	○
8	○	○	○	○
9	○	○	○	○
10	○	○	○	○
11	○	○	○	○
12	○	○	○	○
13	○	○	○	○
14	○	○	○	○
15	○	○	○	○

1. Which figure is formed by assembling the following pieces?

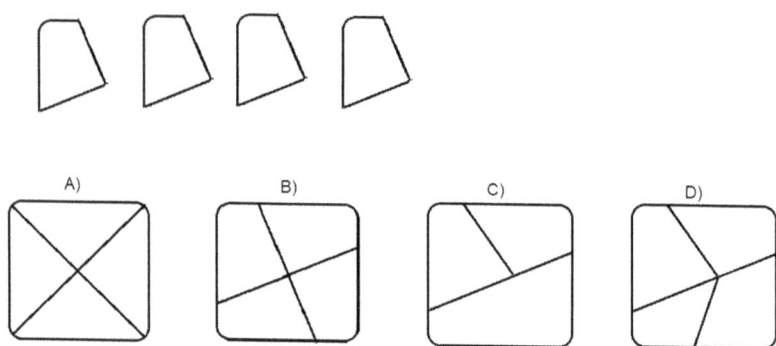

2. Which figure is formed by assembling the following pieces?

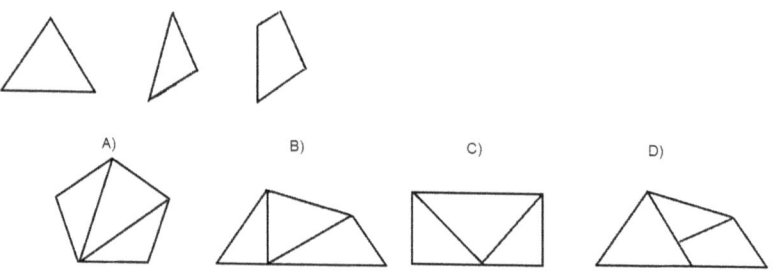

3. Which figure is formed by assembling the following pieces?

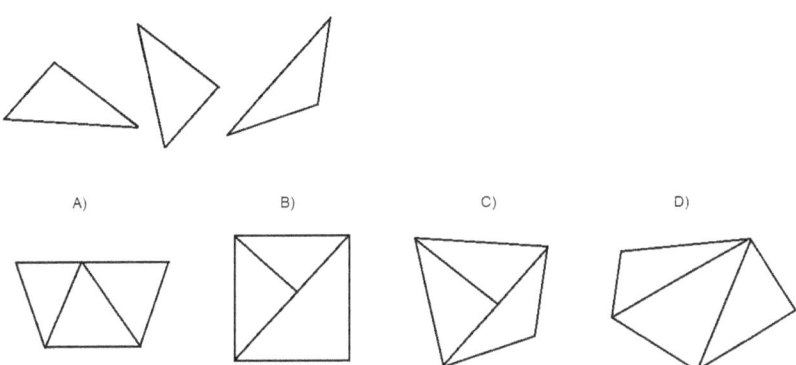

4. Which figure is formed by assembling the following pieces?

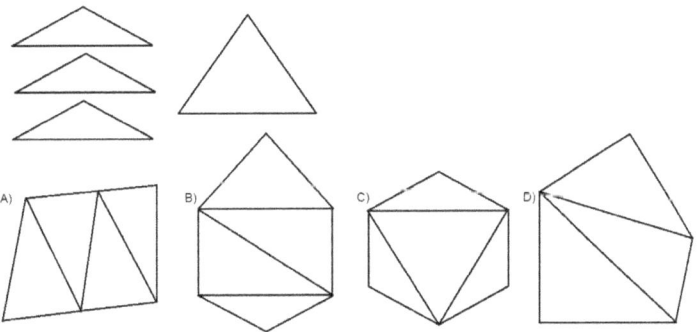

5. Which figure is formed by assembling the following pieces?

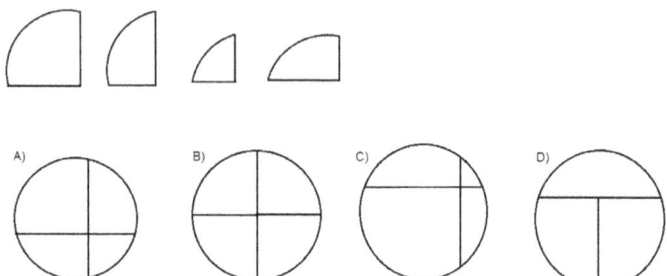

6. Which figure is formed by assembling the following pieces?

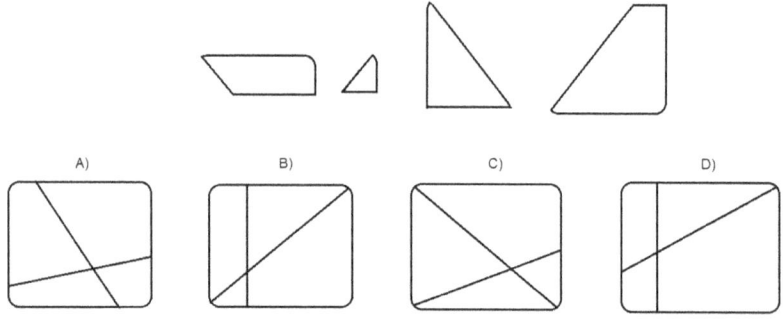

7. Which figure is formed by assembling the following pieces?

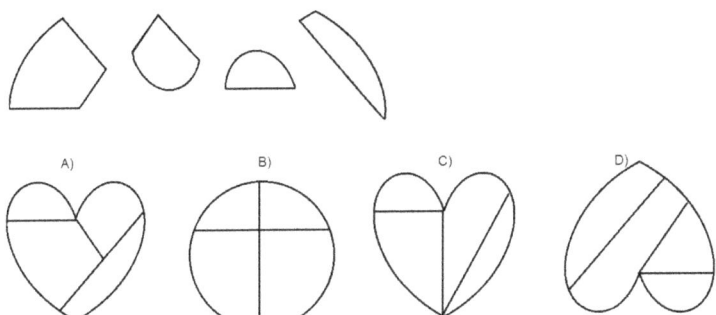

8. Which figure is formed by assembling the following pieces?

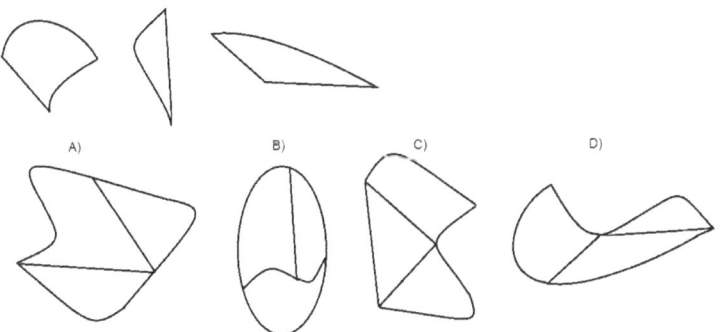

9. Which figure is formed by assembling the following pieces?

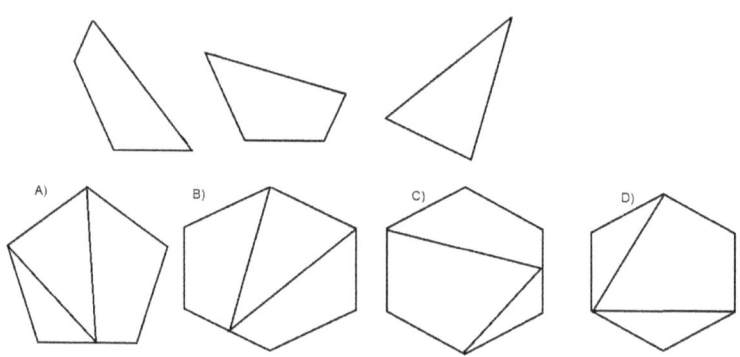

10. Which figure is formed by assembling the following pieces?

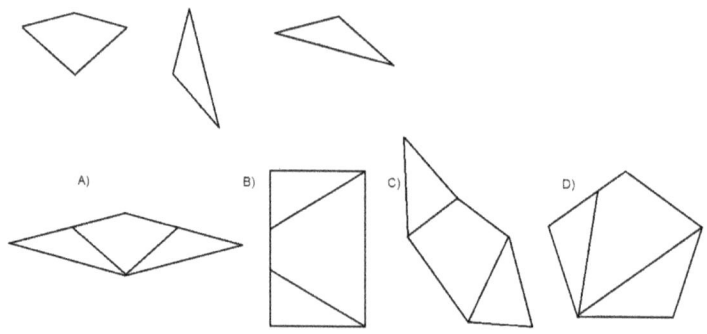

11. Which figure is formed by assembling the following pieces?

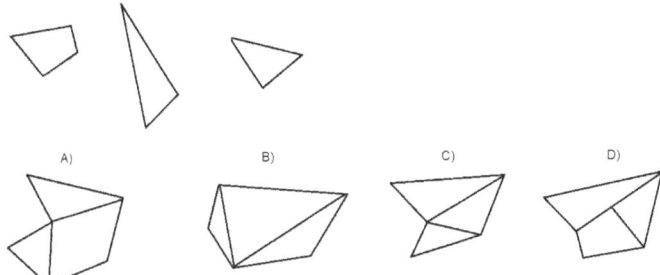

12. Which figure is formed by assembling the following pieces?

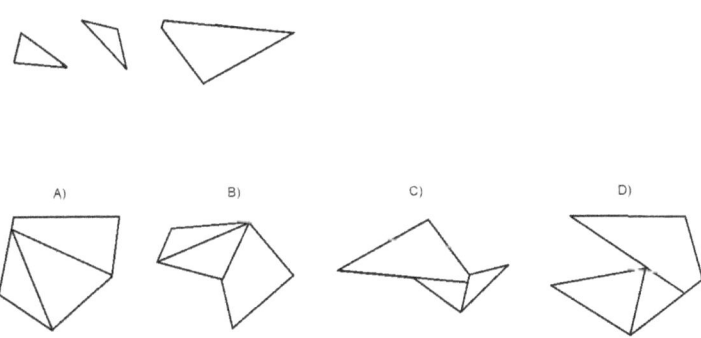

13. Which figure is formed by assembling the following pieces?

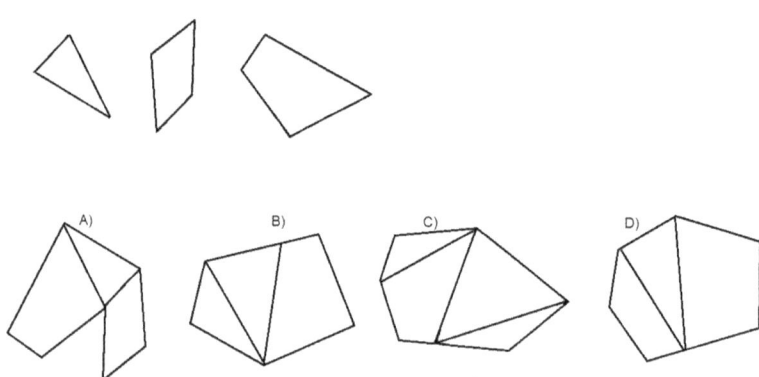

14. Which figure is formed by assembling the following pieces?

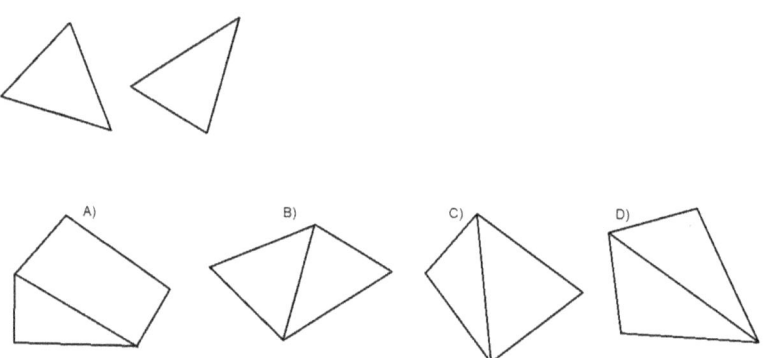

15. Which figure is formed by assembling the following pieces?

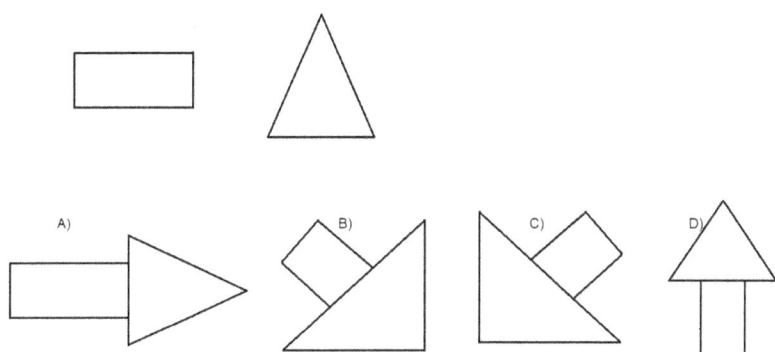

Answer Key

1. B
Since the pieces are identical, only the first two figures can qualify as candidates for the correct answer. The cutting traces in first figure represent the diagonals of the shape. This is not the case here. Hence, only the second figure fits the description.

2. D
There are two triangles and one quadrilateral in the separate pieces. Thus, since all figures except the fourth one contain only triangles, the choice D is the only that fits the description.

3. C
There are two right triangles and one wide triangle in the separate pieces. Only the third figure contains a wide triangle.

4. C
There are three identical right triangles and one equilateral triangle in the separate pieces. Only the third figure contains an equilateral triangle.

5. A
The figure B is excluded as it contains identical pieces. The fourth figure is excluded as well, as it contain only three pieces. So, we have to consider only A and C. The option C contains a very small and a very large piece that are not in the original figure.

6. B
There are two quadrilaterals and two triangles in the original figure. Choice A contains four quadrilaterals, thus it is not the right shape. Choice C contains one quadrilateral and three triangles, and choice D contains three quadrilaterals and one triangle. They are both incorrect.
The only remaining choice is the second one, which contains two quadrilaterals and two triangles.

7. A
Rotating the first piece by 90⁰ anticlockwise, flipping the second piece vertically, and rotating the fourth piece by 90° clockwise, you will obtain the shape shown in the choice A.

8. D
Rotating the first piece by 90⁰ anticlockwise, the second piece by 90⁰ clockwise and the flipping the third piece vertically, you will obtain the figure shown in the choice D.

9. B
Rotating the first and the second shapes by 90⁰ clockwise, and the third shape by 180⁰, you will obtain the figure shown in the choice B.

10. A
The first and the third shape do not need any rotation while the second shape rotates by 90⁰ clockwise. As a result, you will obtain the figure shown in the first option.

11. D
The first shape rotates by 180°, while the second and the third shape by 90⁰ clockwise. As a result, you obtain the fourth figure.

12. C
The first and the third shape rotate by 180⁰, while the second shape rotates by 90⁰ clockwise. As a result, you will obtain choice C.

13. C
The first and the second shape rotate by 180°, while the third shape rotates by 90⁰ anticlockwise.

14. B
Judging by the dimensions and the type of triangles, it is easy to conclude that choice B is the only one that fits the description.

15. A
Judging by the dimensions and the type of shapes, it is easy to conclude that the choice A is the only one that fits the description.

Jigsaw

	A	B	C	D
1	○	○	○	○
2	○	○	○	○
3	○	○	○	○
4	○	○	○	○
5	○	○	○	○
6	○	○	○	○
7	○	○	○	○
8	○	○	○	○
9	○	○	○	○
10	○	○	○	○
11	○	○	○	○
12	○	○	○	○
13	○	○	○	○
14	○	○	○	○
15	○	○	○	○

1. Which option completes the figure below?

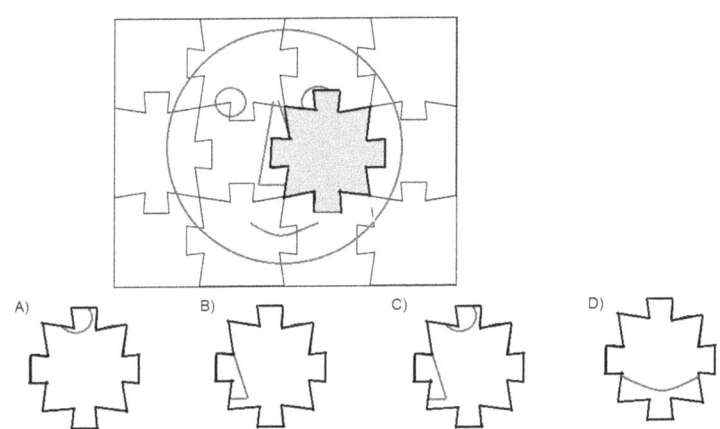

2. Which option completes the figure below?

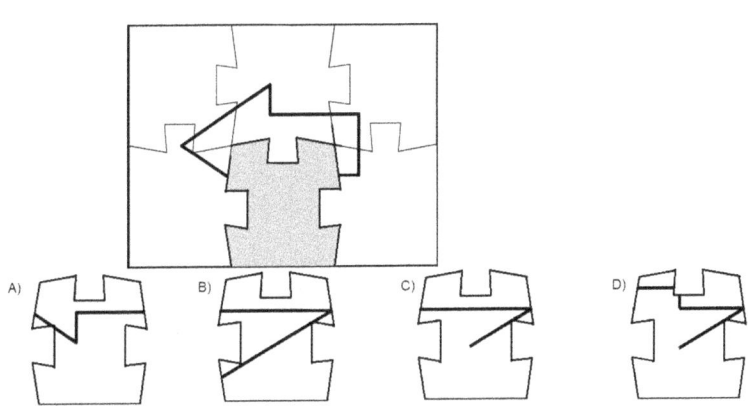

3. Which option completes the figure below?

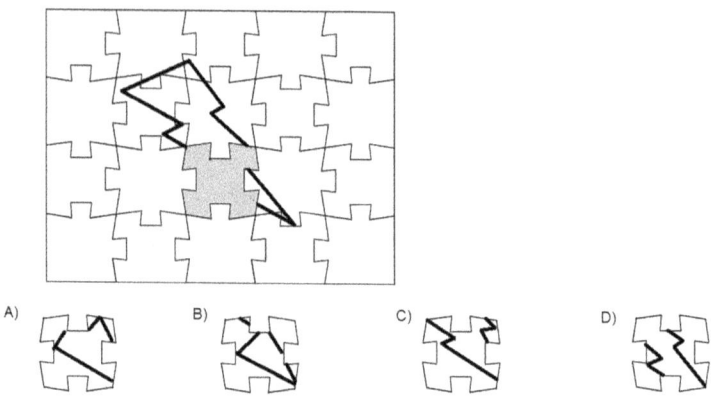

4. Which option completes the figure below?

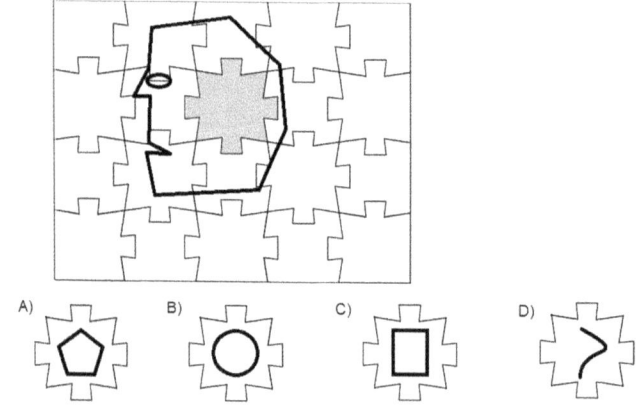

5. Which option completes the figure below?

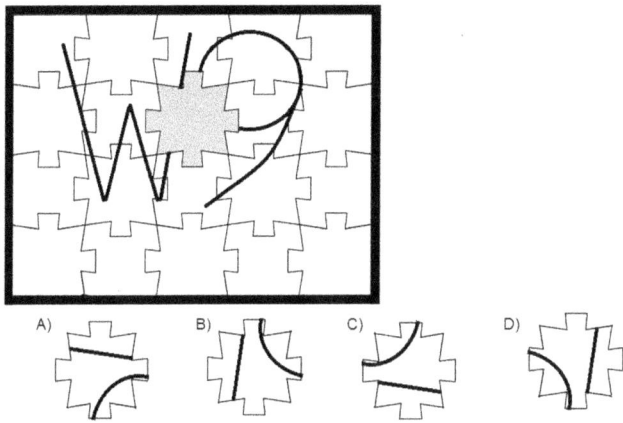

6. Which option completes the figure below?

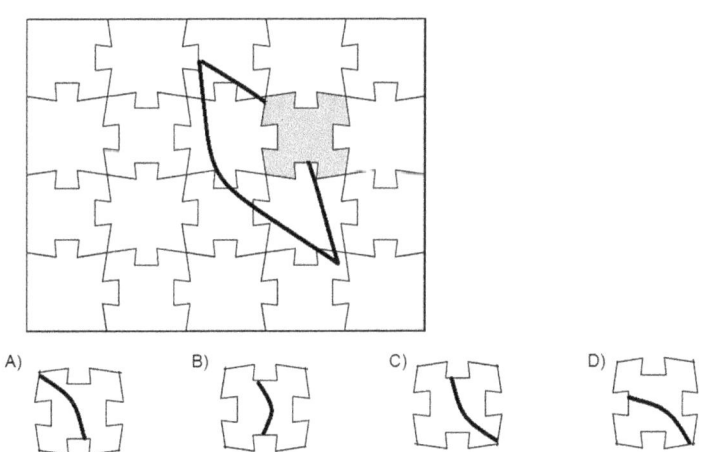

7. Which option completes the figure below?

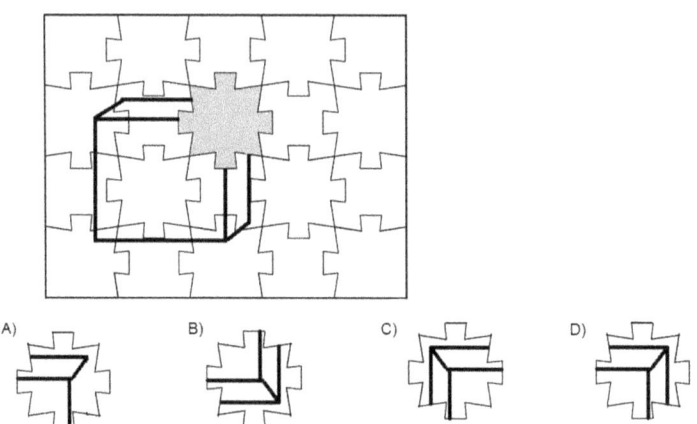

8. Which option completes the figure below?

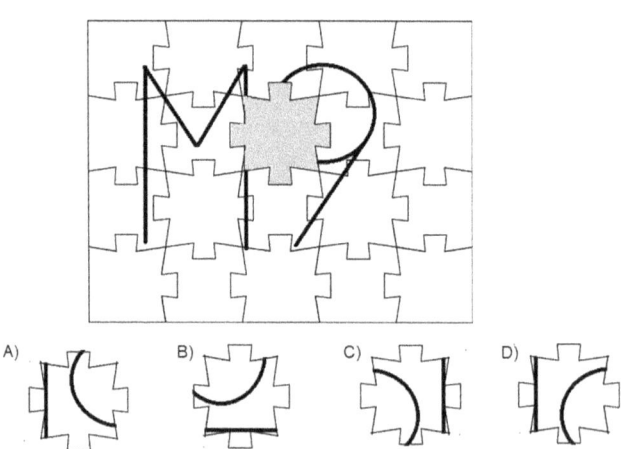

9. Which option completes the figure below?

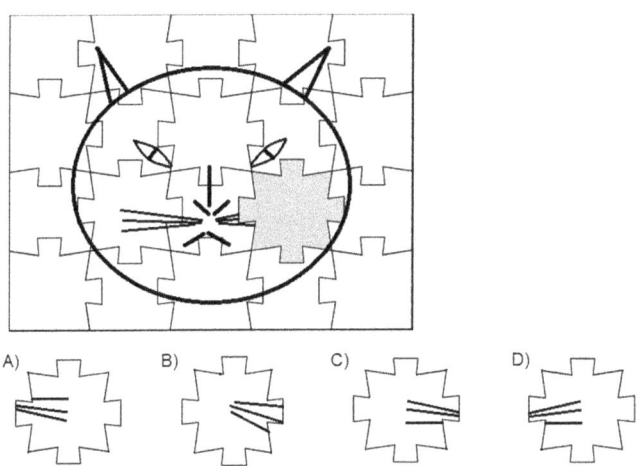

10. Which option completes the figure below?

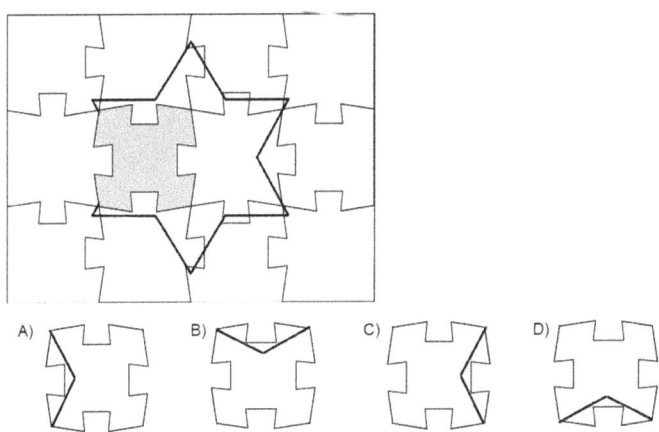

11. Which option completes the figure below?

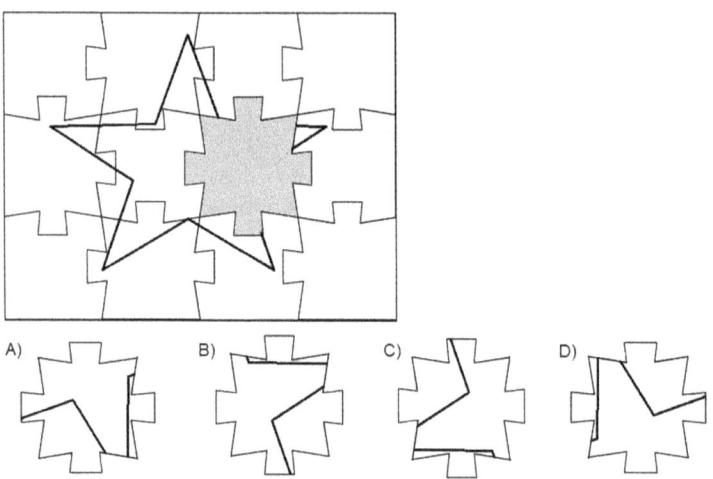

12. Which option completes the figure below?

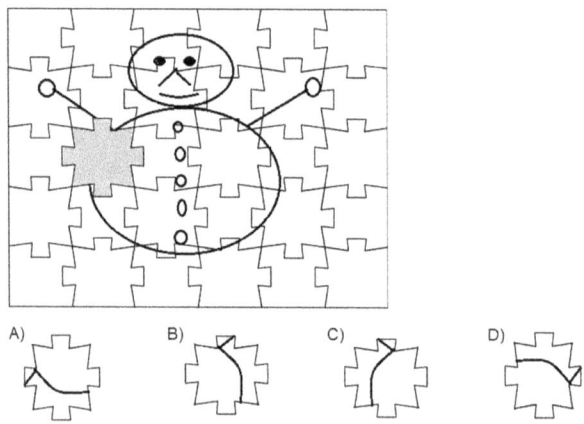

13. Which option completes the figure below?

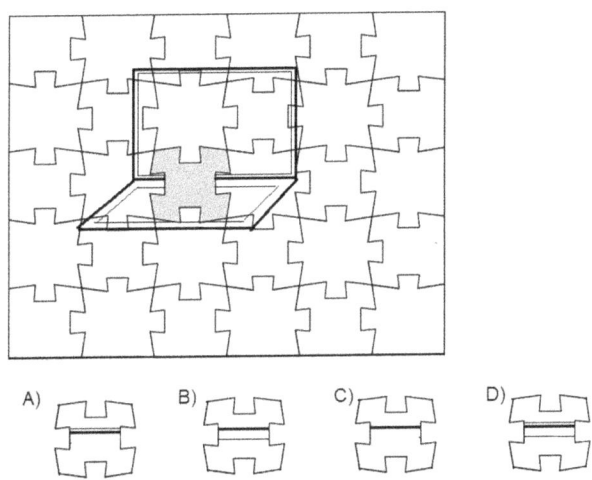

14. Which option completes the figure below?

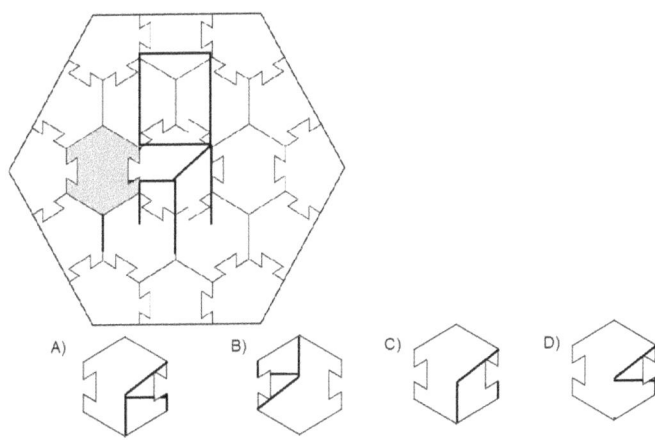

15. **Which option completes the figure below?**

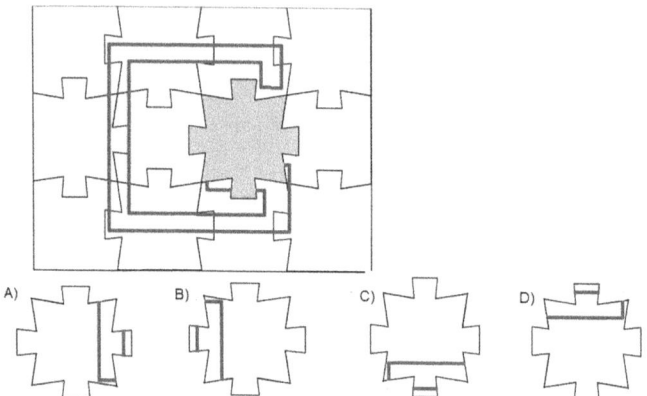

Answer Key

1. C
The figure represents a symmetrical face, with part of the eye and a part of the nose are missing.

The only piece that fits the description is choice C.

2. A
The figure represents a kind of symmetrical horizontal arrow. Therefore, a part of the lateral edge of the tip is missing.

The only piece that fits the description is choice A.

3. C
The figure represents the lightning symbol. You can see that the line interrupts at the upper left corner of the missing piece, so it must continue in that place.

The only piece that fits the description is choice C.

4. D
The figure represents a kind of human head in the lateral position. You can imagine that in the place of missing piece there must be an ear.

The only piece that fits the description is choice D, as the figure is the closest to the ear shape.

5. B
The figure represents a kind of script, more precisely two letters: W and 9. Thus, in the missing piece, there must be a part of W (a line) and a part of the number 9 (a curve).

The only shape that fits the description is choice B.

6. A
The figure represents a kind of tree-leaf-shaped object.

Judging by the leaf symmetry, the missing piece is in choice A.

7. A
The figure represents a 3-D cube. Judging by the cube's symmetry, the missing piece represents the upper-right corner.

8. A
The figure represents a kind of script, more precisely two letters: M and 9. The missing piece, must contain a part of M (a vertical line) and a part of the number 9 (the lower-left part of a circle).

The only shape that fits the description is choice A.

9. D
The figure represents a cat face. The missing piece must contain the right part of the whiskers. Judging by the symmetry of the figure, the whiskers are pointed up (left to right).

The only figure that fits the description is choice D.

10. A
The figure represents a six-pointed star. Judging by the figure's symmetry, choice A represents the missing piece.

11. B
The figure represents a pentacle. The missing piece is the one shown in choice B.

12. C
The figure represents a kind of snowman shape. Thus, by symmetry, the missing piece is choice C.

13. D
The figure resembles to a laptop. The thick line shows the laptop borders and the thin lines represent the screen border and the keyboard border respectively.

The missing shape must contain all of them, choice D.

14. A
The figure resembles to a chair in which the middle left part is missing.

15. C

The figure resembles the letter G with the left part is missing.

Choice C represents the missing piece.

Matching Shapes

	A	B	C	D
1	○	○	○	○
2	○	○	○	○
3	○	○	○	○
4	○	○	○	○
5	○	○	○	○
6	○	○	○	○
7	○	○	○	○
8	○	○	○	○
9	○	○	○	○
10	○	○	○	○
11	○	○	○	○
12	○	○	○	○
13	○	○	○	○
14	○	○	○	○
15	○	○	○	○

Questions 1 - 4 refer to the following figure

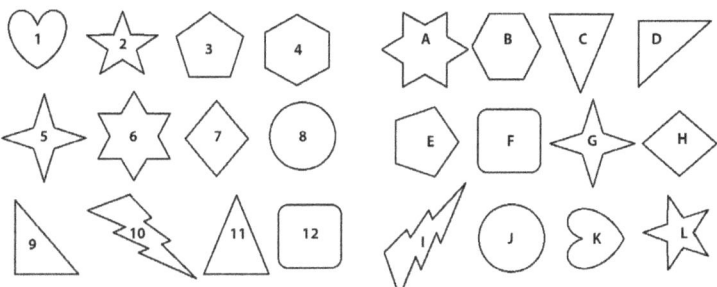

1. Which of the following set of matching pairs are correct?

    a. 1-f   3-g   10-k
    b. 7-c   9-d   1-j
    c. 4-h   11-c   9-d
    d. 8-j   5-g   9-d

2. Which of the following set of matching pairs are correct?

    a. 11-d   6-1   4-e
    b. 12-j   5-1   7-e
    c. 9-d   11-c   6-a
    d. 9-d   2-1   6-1

3. Which of the following set of matching pairs are correct?

    a. 3-1   5-g   2-k
    b. 7-h   3-e   2-l
    c. 6-a   11-d   12-f
    d. 10-i   5-g   4-b

4. Which of the following set of matching pairs are correct?

    a. 7-f   9-c   12-f
    b. 5-l   7-g   9-d
    c. 1-j   12-f   6-l
    d. 5-g   11-c   1-k

Questions 5 - 7 refer to the following figure

5. Which of the following set of matching pairs are correct?

    a. 2-k   7-l   5-b
    b. 11-b   4-e   2-i
    c. 8-g   6-d   10-k
    d. 12j   9-c   3-h

6. Which of the following set of matching pairs are correct?

    a. 1-g   12-j   8-f
    b. 9-c   1-g   5-l
    c. 4-e   5-k   7-c
    d. 6-d   10-a 11-c

7. Which of the following set of matching pairs are correct?

    a. 10-h 8-f   4-l
    b. 10-e 5-d   11-b
    c. 6-d   10-h 12-j
    d. 5-g   7-I   10-a

Questions 8 - 11 refer to the following figure

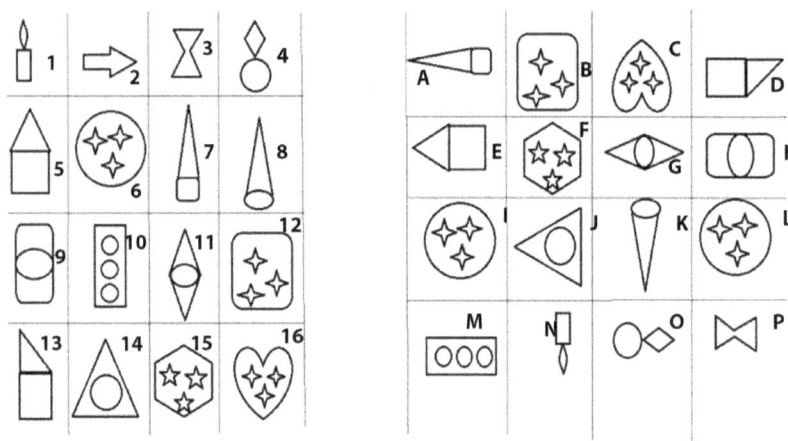

8. Which of the following statements about the shapes in the figure below is correct?

    a. 1, 7, 10 and 16 match with m, j, k, and p respectively

    b. 6, 7, 8 and 13 match with i, a, k and d respectively

    c. 2, 5, 9 and 10 match with b, f, d and e respectively

    d. 4, 10, 11 and 15 match with m, n, o and p respectively

9. Which of the following statements about the shapes in the figure below is correct?

    a. 1, 7, 10 and 16 match with n, a, m, and c respectively

    b. 2, 6, 8 and 12 match with i, a, k and d respectively

    c. 2, 5, 9 and 10 match with c, f, k and e respectively

    d. 4, 10, 11 and 15 match with m, n, o and b respectively

10. Which of the following statements about the shapes in the figure below is correct?

    a. 5, 7, 9 and 11 match with e, g, i and l respectively

    b. 1, 2, 3 and 4 match with a, b, c and d respectively

    c. 13, 14, 15 and 16 match with m, n, o and p respectively

    d. 9, 10, 11 and 12 match with h, m, g and b respectively

11. Which of the following statements about the shapes in the figure below are incorrect?

    a. All shapes on the left part of the figure have a single match on the right part of the figure

    b. The upper row of numbered part of the table corresponds to the second column of the lettered part of the table

    c. 14 corresponds to j but 5 does not correspond to d

    d. The shape n is obtained by turning the shape 1 upside down

Questions 12 - 15 refer to the following figure

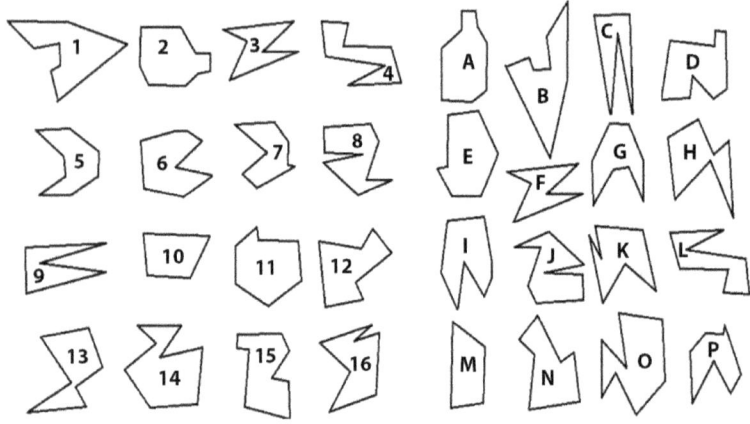

12. Which of the following statements about the shapes in the figure below is correct?

    a. 1, 3, 5 and 16 match with n, a, m, and c respectively

    b. 2, 6, 7 and 12 match with i, a, k and d respectively

    c. 4, 5, 9 and 10 match with c, f, k and e respectively

    d. 5, 6, 9 and 11, match with g, i, c and e respectively

13. Which of the following statements about the shapes in the figure below is correct?

    a. 1, 2, 5 and 6 match with a, b, c and d respectively

    b. 13, 14, 15 and 16 match with d, e, f and m respectively

    c. 2, 10, 11 and 12 match with a, m, e and n respectively

    d. 6, 8, 9 and 10 match with c, f, g and o respectively

MATCHING SHAPES

14. Which of the following statements about the shapes in the figure below is correct?

    a. 9 matches with f but 15 doesn't match with d
    b. 1 matches with b but 15 doesn't match with e
    c. 14 matches with k but 7 doesn't match with g
    d. 10 matches with m but 11 doesn't match with e

15. Which of the following pairs of shapes do NOT match?

    a. 9-c   13-h   16-k
    b. 2-a   6-i   14-o
    c. 13-h 15-d 16-k
    d. 9-c   6-I   4-k

Answer Key

1. D
Choice D is correct as 8 and j both represent circles, 5 and g both represents four pointed stars, while 9 and d both represent right triangles.

2. C
Choice C is correct as 9 and d both represent right triangles, 11 and c both represent isosceles triangles while 6 and both represent six-pointed stars.

3. B
Choice B is correct as 7 and h both represent rhombuses, 3 and e both represent pentagons while 2 and l both represent pentacles.

4. D
Choice D is correct as 5 and g both represent four pointed stars, 11 and c both represent isosceles triangles while 1 and k both represent heart-like shapes.

5. B
Choice B is correct as b is obtained by the 180° rotation of 11, e is obtained by rotating 4 by 180° and i is obtained by a 90° anticlockwise rotation of 2.

6. A
Choice A is correct as g is obtained by rotating 1 by 180°, j is obtained by rotating 12 by 90° anticlockwise and f is obtained by rotating 8 by 90° clockwise.

7. C
Choice C is correct as d is obtained by rotating 6 by 90° anticlockwise, h is obtained by rotating 10 by 180° and j is obtained by rotating the shape 12 by 90° anticlockwise.

8. B
6 matches with i, 7 with a, 8 with k and 13 with d, regardless of the figures' rotation.

9. A
1 matches with n, 7 with a, 10 with m and 16 with c, regardless of the figures' rotation.

10. D
9 matches with h, 10 with m, 11 with g and 12 with b, regardless of the figures' rotation.

11. B
Choice A is correct. Each shape in the left part of the figure has a unique match in the right part.
Choice B is incorrect. The upper row of numbered part of the table does not correspond to the second column of the lettered part of the table.
Choice C is correct. 14 corresponds to j but 5 corresponds to e, not d.
Choice D is correct. The shape n is obtained by turning the shape 1 upside down.

12. D
5 matches with g, 6 with i, 9 with c and 11 with e, regardless of the figures' rotation.

13. C
2 matches with a, 10 with m, 11 with e and 12 with n, regardless of the figures' rotation.

14. B
Choice A is incorrect. 9 does not match with f.
Choice B is correct. 1 matches with b but 15 doesn't match with e.
Choice C is incorrect. 14 does not match with k.
Choice D is incorrect because 11 matches with e.

15. D
All choices match except choice D, 6-l and 4-k.

Visual Comparison

	A	B	C	D
1	○	○	○	○
2	○	○	○	○
3	○	○	○	○
4	○	○	○	○
5	○	○	○	○
6	○	○	○	○
7	○	○	○	○
8	○	○	○	○
9	○	○	○	○
10	○	○	○	○
11	○	○	○	○
12	○	○	○	○
13	○	○	○	○
14	○	○	○	○
15	○	○	○	○

1. Which figure has the greatest shaded area?

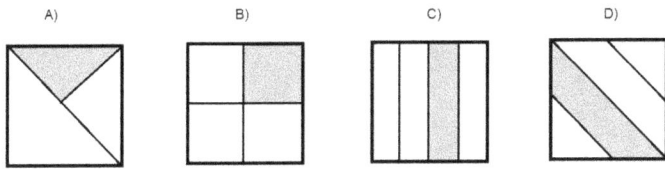

2. Which figure need less color to paint?

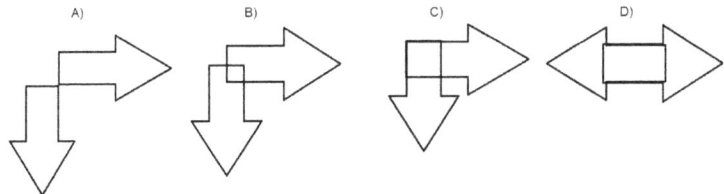

3. Which figure has the smallest shaded area?

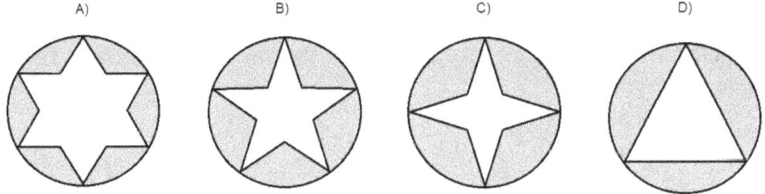

4. Which figure has the smallest shaded area?

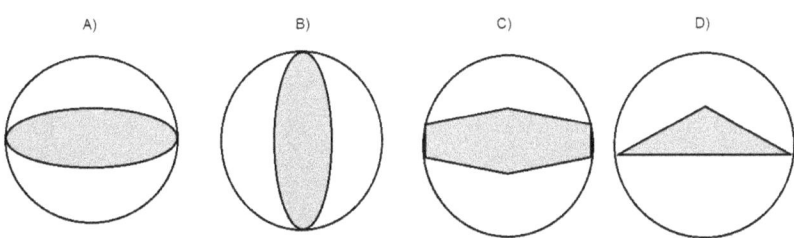

5. Which gear requires more material to produce?

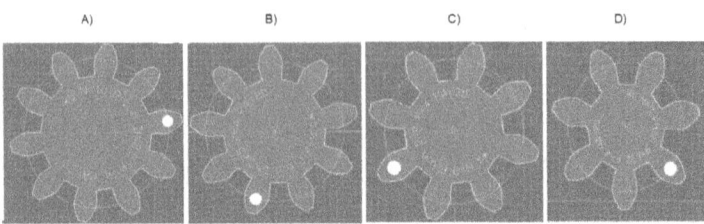

6. Which triangle will hold the largest inscribed circle?

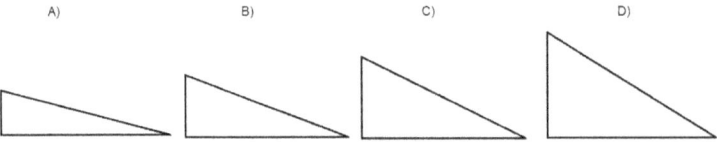

7. Which figure has the greatest space between the two shapes?

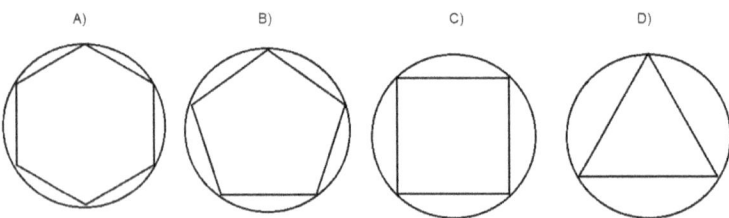

8. Which figure will hold the largest inscribed circle?

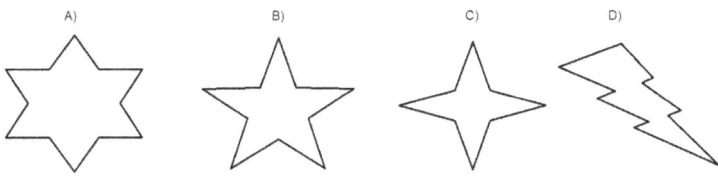

9. Which figure below will take the greatest amount of wire?

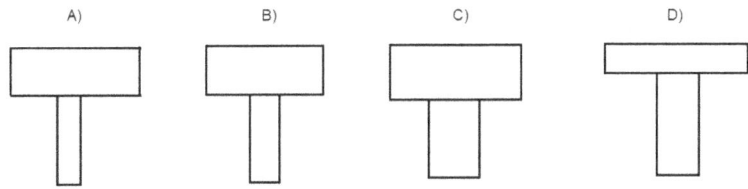

10. Which of the shapes below is the smallest?

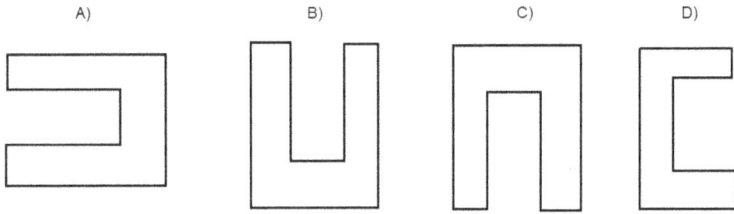

11. Which flower below is the biggest?

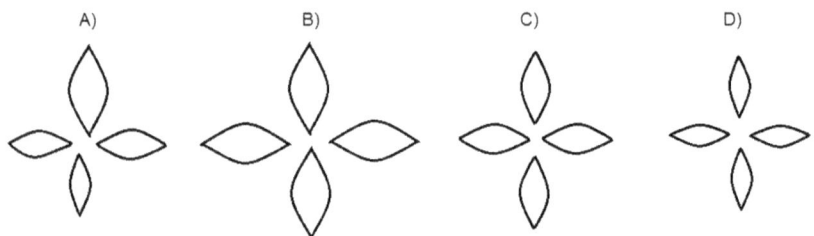

12. If the shapes shown below are made of metal, which shape uses a greater amount of metal?

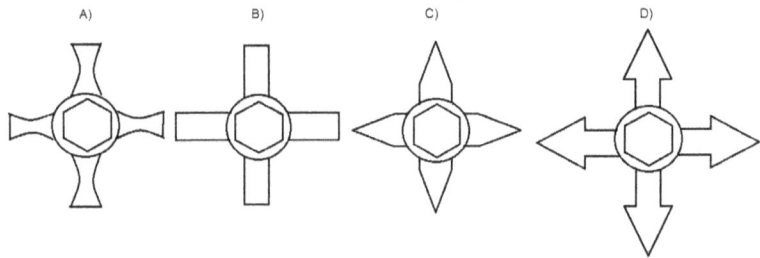

13. Which shape below uses the most paint?

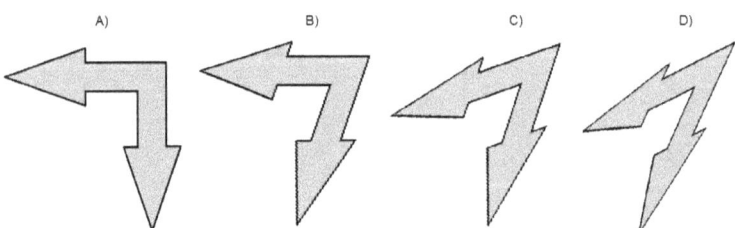

14. Which figure will hold the largest inscribed circle?

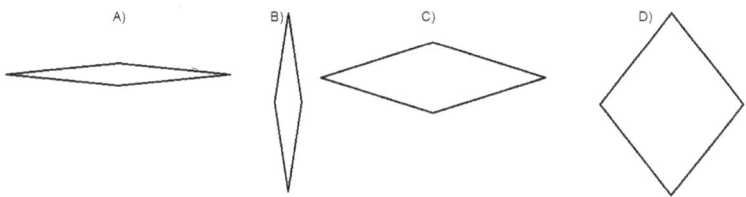

15. Which of the inscribed figures below is the smallest?

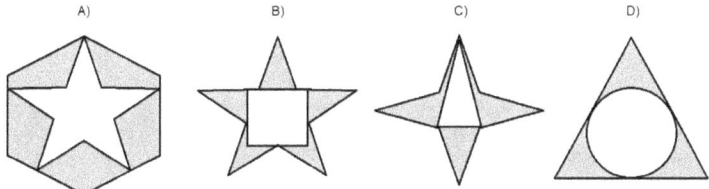

Answer Key

1. D
In the first three figures, one quarter is shaded. Only choice D has a shaded area greater than one quarter.

2. D
The figure that needs the least paint is the one with the smallest surface area. In choice D, the arrows overlap the most, so the surface area is the smallest and requires the least paint.

3. A
Figure A has the most white space. Since all the circles are identical, the shaded area of the first figure is the smallest.

4. D
Choice D has more white space than the other shapes. Since all the circles are identical, the shaded area of choice D (the triangle) is the smallest.

5. A
Choice A has a greater internal diameter (without including the teeth), and has more teeth, and therefore requires more material to produce.

6. D
Choice D is the largest triangle and will hold the largest inscribed circle.

7. D
Choice D has more space between the inner shape (triangle) and the outer shape (circle).

8. A
Choice A has the largest interior volume and can contain the largest inscribed circle.

9. C
The larger the rectangles that make up the figure, the more wire will be required. Choice C has the largest area, and requires the most wire to produce.

10. D
The first three shapes have one short and two long sides. Choice D is the smallest, with one long and two short sides.

11. B
Choice A has 1 small, 2 medium, and one large petal.
Choice B is the largest, with 4 large petals.
Choice C has 4 medium size petals.
Choice D has 4 small petals.

12. D
Looking carefully at the dimensions and thickness of the figures, choice D is the largest and will take the most material to produce.

13. A
When the angle between the arrows decreases, their thickness also decreases. So the largest dimension (choice A) will be when the angle is $90°$.

14. D
The wider the figure, the larger the inscribed circle. Therefore, choice A will contain the largest inscribed circle.

15. C
Choice C is correct. Choice B and C are very similar, however, since for similar dimensions a triangle, has a smaller area than a rectangle, the hesitation perishes.

Conclusion

CONGRATULATIONS! You have made it this far because you have applied yourself diligently to practicing for the exam and no doubt improved your potential score considerably! Getting into a good school is a huge step in a journey that might be challenging at times but will be many times more rewarding and fulfilling. That is why being prepared is so important.

Good Luck!

www.ingramcontent.com/pod-product-compliance
Lightning Source LLC
LaVergne TN
LVHW010302260326
834688LV00044B/1410